W0009639

DOVER · THRIFT · EDITIONS

My Last Duchess and Other Poems

ROBERT BROWNING

DOVER PUBLICATIONS, INC.
New York

DOVER THRIFT EDITIONS

GENERAL EDITOR: STANLEY APPELBAUM
EDITOR OF THIS VOLUME: SHANE WELLER

Copyright

Copyright © 1993 by Dover Publications, Inc.
All rights reserved under Pan American and International Copyright Conventions.

Published in Canada by General Publishing Company, Ltd., 30 Lesmill Road, Don Mills, Toronto, Ontario.
Published in the United Kingdom by Constable and Company, Ltd., 3 The Lanchesters, 162–164 Fulham Palace Road, London W6 9ER.

Bibliographical Note

This Dover edition, first published in 1993, is a new selection of poems, reprinted from *Poems of Robert Browning*, published by Thomas Y. Crowell & Company, New York, in 1896; and *The Poems of Robert Browning*, published by Oxford University Press, London, in 1905. The Note, footnotes and the alphabetical lists of titles and first lines have been prepared specially for the present edition.

Library of Congress Cataloging-in-Publication Data

Browning, Robert, 1812–1889.
   My last duchess, and other poems / Robert Browning.
      p.   cm. — (Dover thrift editions)
   ISBN 0-486-27783-6 (pbk.)
   I. Title. II. Series.
PR4202.D68   1993
821'.8—dc20   93-22085
                                                CIP

Manufactured in the United States of America
Dover Publications, Inc., 31 East 2nd Street, Mineola, N.Y. 11501

Note

ROBERT BROWNING (1812–1889) stands alongside Tennyson as one of the colossi of Victorian poetry; yet, owing partly to the formal and linguistic complexity of his work, partly to his use of rich topographical and historical detail, he achieved recognition only late in life, with the publication of the dauntingly elaborate *The Ring and the Book* (1868–69), an ambitious fusion of novel, drama and epic poem. Among his most noteworthy collections of shorter verse are *Dramatic Lyrics* (1842), *Dramatic Romances and Lyrics* (1845), *Men and Women* (1855) and *Dramatis Personae* (1864). Browning began his literary career as a dramatist, and although his plays are now little read, he is celebrated for having created the poetic form known as the dramatic monologue, among which some of his best known are "My Last Duchess," "Fra Lippo Lippi" and "Andrea del Sarto." Besides these poems, the present selection also includes many of the other high points from throughout the writer's creative life, among which are the narrative children's poem "The Pied Piper of Hamelin"; the famous attack on Wordsworth, "The Lost Leader"; the love poems "Meeting at Night" and "The Last Ride Together"; and the lyric "Home-Thoughts from Abroad." The song from *Pippa Passes*, perhaps Browning's most well-known piece of verse, is the only extract included here.

Contents

(The date following the title of an individual poem indicates
first publication when this does not coincide with the poem's
appearance in the collection under which it is listed.)

My Last Duchess
and Other Poems

Song

The year's at the spring,
And day's at the morn;
Morning's at seven;
The hill-side's dew-pearled;
The lark's on the wing;
The snail's on the thorn;
God's in His heaven—
All's right with the world!

My Last Duchess

FERRARA

That's my last Duchess painted on the wall,
Looking as if she were alive. I call
That piece a wonder, now: Frà Pandolf's hands
Worked busily a day, and there she stands.
Will 't please you sit and look at her? I said
"Frà Pandolf" by design: for never read
Strangers like you that pictured countenance,
The depth and passion of its earnest glance,
But to myself they turned (since none puts by
The curtain I have drawn for you, but I)
And seemed as they would ask me, if they durst,
How such a glance came there; so, not the first
Are you to turn and ask thus. Sir, 't was not
Her husband's presence only, called that spot
Of joy into the Duchess' cheek: perhaps
Frà Pandolf chanced to say "Her mantle laps
Over my lady's wrist too much," or "Paint
Must never hope to reproduce the faint
Half-flush that dies along her throat:" such stuff
Was courtesy, she thought, and cause enough

1

For calling up that spot of joy. She had
A heart—how shall I say?—too soon made glad,
Too easily impressed; she liked whate'er
She looked on, and her looks went everywhere.
Sir, 't was all one! My favour at her breast,
The dropping of the daylight in the West,
The bough of cherries some officious fool
Broke in the orchard for her, the white mule
She rode with round the terrace—all and each
Would draw from her alike the approving speech,
Or blush, at least. She thanked men,—good! but thanked
Somehow—I know not how—as if she ranked
My gift of a nine-hundred-years-old name
With anybody's gift. Who'd stoop to blame
This sort of trifling? Even had you skill
In speech—(which I have not)—to make your will
Quite clear to such an one, and say, "Just this
Or that in you disgusts me; here you miss,
Or there exceed the mark"—and if she let
Herself be lessoned so, nor plainly set
Her wits to yours, forsooth, and made excuse,
—E'en then would be some stooping; and I choose
Never to stoop. Oh sir, she smiled, no doubt,
Whene'er I passed her; but who passed without
Much the same smile? This grew; I gave commands;
Then all smiles stopped together. There she stands
As if alive. Will 't please you rise? We'll meet
The company below, then. I repeat,
The Count your master's known munificence
Is ample warrant that no just pretence
Of mine for dowry will be disallowed;
Though his fair daughter's self, as I avowed
At starting, is my object. Nay, we'll go
Together down, sir. Notice Neptune, though,
Taming a sea-horse, thought a rarity,
Which Claus of Innsbruck cast in bronze for me!

Incident of the French Camp

I   You know, we French stormed Ratisbon:
     A mile or so away
On a little mound, Napoleon
     Stood on our storming-day;
With neck out-thrust, you fancy how,
     Legs wide, arms locked behind,
As if to balance the prone brow
     Oppressive with its mind.

II   Just as perhaps he mused "My plans
     That soar, to earth may fall,
Let once my army-leader Lannes
     Waver at yonder wall"—
Out 'twixt the battery-smokes there flew
     A rider, bound on bound
Full-galloping; nor bridle drew
     Until he reached the mound.

III   Then off there flung in smiling joy,
     And held himself erect
By just his horse's mane, a boy:
     You hardly could suspect—
(So tight he kept his lips compressed,
     Scarce any blood came through)
You looked twice ere you saw his breast
     Was all but shot in two.

IV   "Well," cried he, "Emperor, by God's grace
     We've got you Ratisbon!
The Marshal's in the market-place,
     And you'll be there anon
To see your flag-bird flap his vans[1]
     Where I, to heart's desire,
Perched him!" The chief's eye flashed; his plans
     Soared up again like fire.

---

[1] Wings.

v   The chief's eye flashed; but presently
      Softened itself, as sheathes
A film the mother-eagle's eye
      When her bruised eaglet breathes.
"You're wounded!" "Nay," the soldier's pride
      Touched to the quick, he said:
"I'm killed, Sire!" And his chief beside,
      Smiling the boy fell dead.

Soliloquy of the Spanish Cloister

I   Gr-r-r—there go, my heart's abhorrence!
      Water your damned flower-pots, do!
If hate killed men, Brother Lawrence,
      God's blood, would not mine kill you!
What? your myrtle-bush wants trimming?
      Oh, that rose has prior claims—
Needs its leaden vase filled brimming?
      Hell dry you up with its flames!

II   At the meal we sit together:
      Salve tibi![1] I must hear
Wise talk of the kind of weather,
      Sort of season, time of year:
Not a plenteous cork-crop: scarcely
      Dare we hope oak-galls, I doubt:
What's the Latin name for "parsley"?
      What's the Greek name for Swine's Snout?[2]

III   Whew! We'll have our platter burnished,
      Laid with care on our own shelf!
With a fire-new spoon we're furnished,
      And a goblet for ourself,
Rinsed like something sacrificial
      Ere 't is fit to touch our chaps—

---

[1] "Hail to thee!"
[2] Dandelion.

Marked with L for our initial!
(He-he! There his lily snaps!)

IV   *Saint*, forsooth! While brown Dolores
    Squats outside the Convent bank
With Sanchicha, telling stories,
    Steeping tresses in the tank,
Blue-black, lustrous, thick like horse hairs,
    —Can't I see his dead eye glow,
Bright as 't were a Barbary corsair's?
    (That is, if he'd let it show!)

V   When he finishes refection,
    Knife and fork he never lays
Cross-wise, to my recollection,
    As do I, in Jesu's praise.
I the Trinity illustrate,
    Drinking watered orange-pulp—
In three sips the Arian[1] frustrate;
    While he drains his at one gulp.

VI   Oh, those melons? If he's able
    We're to have a feast: so nice!
One goes to the Abbot's table,
    All of us get each a slice.
How go on your flowers? None double?
    Not one fruit-sort can you spy?
Strange!—And I, too, at such trouble
    Keep them close-nipped on the sly!

VII   There's a great text in Galatians
    Once you trip on it, entails
Twenty-nine distinct damnations
    One sure, if another fails:
If I trip him just a-dying,
    Sure of heaven as sure can be,
Spin him round and send him flying
    Off to hell, a Manichee?

---

[1] Follower of Arius, a theologian who denied the doctrine of the Trinity.

VIII   Or, my scrofulous French novel
     On gray paper with blunt type!
Simply glance at it, you grovel
     Hand and foot in Belial's gripe:
If I double down its pages
     At the woeful sixteenth print,
When he gathers his greengages,
     Ope a sieve and slip it in 't?

IX   Or, there's Satan!—one might venture
     Pledge one's soul to him, yet leave
Such a flaw in the indenture
     As he'd miss, till, past retrieve,
Blasted lay that rose-acacia
     We're so proud of! *Hy, Zy, Hine* . . .
'St, there's Vespers! *Plena gratiâ
Ave, Virgo!*[1] Gr-r-r—you swine!

Johannes Agricola in Meditation[2]

There's heaven above, and night by night,
     I look right through its gorgeous roof;
No suns and moons though e'er so bright
     Avail to stop me; splendour-proof
I keep the broods of stars aloof:
For I intend to get to God,
     For 'tis to God I speed so fast,
For in God's breast, my own abode,
     Those shoals of dazzling glory, past,
I lay my spirit down at last.
I lie where I have always lain,
     God smiles as He has always smiled;
Ere suns and moons could wax and wane,
     Ere stars were thundergirt, or piled

---

[1] "Full of grace/Hail, Virgin!"
[2] Johannes Agricola (1494–1566) was the founder of Antinomianism, holding that salvation and damnation are predetermined for individuals.

The heavens, God thought on me His child;
Ordained a life for me, arrayed
   Its circumstances, every one
To the minutest; ay, God said
   This head this hand should rest upon
Thus, ere He fashioned star or sun.
And having thus created me,
   Thus rooted me, He bade me grow,
Guiltless for ever, like a tree
   That buds and blooms, nor seeks to know
   The law by which it prospers so:
But sure that thought and word and deed
   All go to swell His love for me,
Me, made because that love had need
   Of something irrevocably
Pledged solely its content to be.
Yes, yes, a tree which must ascend,
   No poison-gourd foredoomed to stoop!
I have God's warrant, could I blend
   All hideous sins, as in a cup,
To drink the mingled venoms up,
Secure my nature will convert
   The draught to blossoming gladness fast,
While sweet dews turn to the gourd's hurt,
   And bloat, and while they bloat it, blast,
As from the first its lot was cast.
For as I lie, smiled on, full fed
   By unexhausted power to bless,
I gaze below on Hell's fierce bed,
   And those its waves of flame oppress,
Swarming in ghastly wretchedness;
Whose life on earth aspired to be
   One altar-smoke, so pure!—to win
If not love like God's love to me,
   At least to keep His anger in;
And all their striving turned to sin.
   Priest, doctor, hermit, monk grown white
With prayer, the broken-hearted nun,
   The martyr, the wan acolyte,
The incense-swinging child,—undone
Before God fashioned star or sun!

God, whom I praise; how could I praise,
    If such as I might understand,
Make out and reckon on His ways,
    And bargain for His love, and stand,
Paying a price, at His right hand?

Porphyria's Lover

I   The rain set early in to-night,
        The sullen wind was soon awake,
    It tore the elm-tops down for spite,
        And did its worst to vex the lake:
    I listened with heart fit to break.

II   When glided in Porphyria; straight
        She shut the cold out and the storm,
    And kneeled and made the cheerless grate
        Blaze up, and all the cottage warm;
    Which done, she rose, and from her form

III   Withdrew the dripping cloak and shawl,
        And laid her soiled gloves by, untied
    Her hat and let the damp hair fall,
        And, last, she sat down by my side
    And called me. When no voice replied,

IV   She put my arm about her waist,
        And made her smooth white shoulder bare,
    And all her yellow hair displaced,
        And, stooping, made my cheek lie there,
    And spread, o'er all, her yellow hair,

V   Murmuring how she loved me—she
        Too weak, for all her heart's endeavour,
    To set its struggling passion free
        From pride, and vainer ties dissever,
    And give herself to me for ever.

VI   But passion sometimes would prevail,
      Nor could to-night's gay feast restrain
   A sudden thought of one so pale
      For love of her, and all in vain:
   So, she was come thro' wind and rain.

VII   Be sure I looked up at her eyes
      Happy and proud; at last I knew
   Porphyria worshiped me; surprise
      Made my heart swell, and still it grew
   While I debated what to do.

VIII   That moment she was mine, mine, fair,
      Perfectly pure and good: I found
   A thing to do, and all her hair
      In one long yellow string I wound
   Three times her little throat around,

IX   And strangled her. No pain felt she;
      I am quite sure she felt no pain.
   As a shut bud that holds a bee,
      I warily oped her lids: again
   Laughed the blue eyes without a stain.

X   And I untightened next the tress
      About her neck; her cheek once more
   Blushed bright beneath my burning kiss:
      I propped her head up as before.
   Only, this time my shoulder bore

XI   Her head, which droops upon it still:
      The smiling rosy little head,
   So glad it has its utmost will,
      That all it scorned at once is fled,
   And I, its love, am gained instead!

XII   Porphyria's love: she guessed not how
      Her darling one wish would be heard.
   And thus we sit together now.
      And all night long we have not stirred,
   And yet God has not said a word!

The Pied Piper of Hamelin

A CHILD'S STORY

(Written for, and inscribed to, W. M. the Younger)

I   Hamelin Town's in Brunswick,
By famous Hanover city;
   The river Weser, deep and wide,
   Washes its wall on the southern side;
   A pleasanter spot you never spied;
But, when begins my ditty,
   Almost five hundred years ago,
   To see the townsfolk suffer so
     From vermin, was a pity.

II   Rats!
They fought the dogs, and killed the cats,
   And bit the babies in the cradles,
And ate the cheeses out of the vats,
   And licked the soup from the cooks' own ladles,
Split open the kegs of salted sprats,
Made nests inside men's Sunday hats,
And even spoiled the women's chats,
     By drowning their speaking
     With shrieking and squeaking
In fifty different sharps and flats.

III   At last the people in a body
   To the Town Hall came flocking:
' 'Tis clear,' cried they, 'our Mayor's a noddy;
   And as for our Corporation—shocking
To think we buy gowns lined with ermine
For dolts that can't or won't determine
What's best to rid us of our vermin!
You hope, because you're old and obese,
To find in the furry civic robe ease?
Rouse up, Sirs! Give your brains a racking
To find the remedy we're lacking,

Or, sure as fate, we'll send you packing!'
At this the Mayor and Corporation
Quaked with a mighty consternation.

IV An hour they sate in council,
   At length the Mayor broke silence:
'For a guilder I'd my ermine gown sell;
   I wish I were a mile hence!
It's easy to bid one rack one's brain—
I'm sure my poor head aches again
I've scratched it so, and all in vain.
Oh for a trap, a trap, a trap!'
Just as he said this, what should hap
At the chamber door but a gentle tap?
'Bless us,' cried the Mayor, 'what's that?'
(With the Corporation as he sat,
Looking little though wondrous fat;
Nor brighter was his eye, nor moister
Than a too-long-opened oyster,
Save when at noon his paunch grew mutinous
For a plate of turtle green and glutinous)
'Only a scraping of shoes on the mat?
Anything like the sound of a rat
Makes my heart go pit-a-pat!'

V 'Come in!'—the Mayor cried, looking bigger:
And in did come the strangest figure!
His queer long coat from heel to head
Was half of yellow and half of red;
And he himself was tall and thin,
With sharp blue eyes, each like a pin,
And light loose hair, yet swarthy skin,
No tuft on cheek nor beard on chin,
But lips where smiles went out and in—
There was no guessing his kith and kin!
And nobody could enough admire
The tall man and his quaint attire:
Quoth one: 'It's as my great-grandsire,
Starting up at the Trump of Doom's tone,
Had walked this way from his painted tomb-stone!'

VI   He advanced to the council-table:
     And, 'Please your honours,' said he, 'I'm able,
     By means of a secret charm to draw
     All creatures living beneath the sun,
     That creep or swim or fly or run,
     After me so as you never saw!
     And I chiefly use my charm
     On creatures that do people harm,
     The mole and toad and newt and viper;
     And people call me the Pied Piper.'
     (And here they noticed round his neck
     A scarf of red and yellow stripe,
     To match with his coat of the self-same cheque;
     And at the scarf's end hung a pipe;
     And his fingers, they noticed, were ever straying
     As if impatient to be playing
     Upon this pipe, as low it dangled
     Over his vesture so old-fangled.)
     'Yet,' said he, 'poor piper as I am,
     In Tartary I freed the Cham,
     Last June, from his huge swarms of gnats;
     I eased in Asia the Nizam[1]
     Of a monstrous brood of vampyre-bats:
     And as for what your brain bewilders,
     If I can rid your town of rats
     Will you give me a thousand guilders?'
     'One? fifty thousand!'—was the exclamation
     Of the astonished Mayor and Corporation.

VII Into the street the Piper stept,
        Smiling first a little smile,
     As if he knew what magic slept
        In his quiet pipe the while;
     Then, like a musical adept,
     To blow the pipe his lips he wrinkled,
     And green and blue his sharp eyes twinkled
     Like a candle-flame where salt is sprinkled;
     And ere three shrill notes the pipe uttered,

---

[1] The ruler of Hyderabad, in India.

You heard as if an army muttered;
And the muttering grew to a grumbling;
And the grumbling grew to a mighty rumbling;
And out of the houses the rats came tumbling.
Great rats, small rats, lean rats, brawny rats,
Brown rats, black rats, grey rats, tawny rats,
Grave old plodders, gay young friskers,
    Fathers, mothers, uncles, cousins,
Cocking tails and pricking whiskers,
    Families by tens and dozens,
Brothers, sisters, husbands, wives—
Followed the Piper for their lives.
From street to street he piped advancing,
And step for step they followed dancing,
Until they came to the river Weser
Wherein all plunged and perished!
—Save one who, stout as Julius Caesar,
Swam across and lived to carry
(As he, the manuscript he cherished)
To Rat-land home his commentary:
Which was, 'At the first shrill notes of the pipe,
I heard a sound as of scraping tripe,
And putting apples, wondrous ripe,
Into a cider-press's gripe:
And a moving away of pickle-tub-boards,
And a leaving ajar of conserve-cupboards,
And a drawing the corks of train-oil-flasks, [1]
And a breaking the hoops of butter-casks;
And it seemed as if a voice
(Sweeter far than by harp or by psaltery
Is breathed) called out, Oh rats, rejoice!
The world is grown to one vast drysaltery!
So, munch on, crunch on, take your nuncheon, [2]
Breakfast, supper, dinner, luncheon!
And just as a bulky sugar-puncheon, [3]
All ready staved, like a great sun shone
Glorious scarce an inch before me,

---

[1] Containing whale oil.
[2] Light meal.
[3] Large cask.

Just as methought it said, Come, bore me!
—I found the Weser rolling o'er me.'

VIII   You should have heard the Hamelin people
Ringing the bells till they rocked the steeple.
'Go,' cried the Mayor, 'and get long poles!
Poke out the nests and block up the holes!
Consult with carpenters and builders,
And leave in our town not even a trace
Of the rats!'—when suddenly, up the face
Of the Piper perked in the market-place,
With a, 'First, if you please, my thousand guilders!'

IX   A thousand guilders! The Mayor looked blue;
So did the Corporation too.
For council dinners made rare havoc
With Claret, Moselle, Vin-de-Grave, Hock;
And half the money would replenish
Their cellar's biggest butt with Rhenish.
To pay this sum to a wandering fellow
With a gipsy coat of red and yellow!
'Beside,' quoth the Mayor with a knowing wink,
'Our business was done at the river's brink;
We saw with our eyes the vermin sink,
And what's dead can't come to life, I think.
So, friend, we're not the folks to shrink
From the duty of giving you something for drink,
And a matter of money to put in your poke;
But as for the guilders, what we spoke
Of them, as you very well know, was in joke.
Beside, our losses have made us thrifty.
A thousand guilders! Come, take fifty!'

X   The piper's face fell, and he cried,
'No trifling! I can't wait, beside!
I've promised to visit by dinner time
Bagdat, and accept the prime
Of the Head-Cook's pottage, all he's rich in,
For having left, in the Caliph's kitchen,
Of a nest of scorpions no survivor—
With him I proved no bargain-driver,

With you, don't think I'll bate a stiver![1]
And folks who put me in a passion
May find me pipe to another fashion.'

XI   'How?' cried the Mayor, 'd'ye think I'll brook
Being worse treated than a Cook?
Insulted by a lazy ribald
With idle pipe and vesture piebald?
You threaten us, fellow? Do your worst,
Blow your pipe there till you burst!'

XII   Once more he stept into the street;
    And to his lips again
Laid his long pipe of smooth straight cane;
    And ere he blew three notes (such sweet
Soft notes as yet musician's cunning
    Never gave the enraptured air)
There was a rustling, that seemed like a bustling
Of merry crowds justling at pitching and hustling,
Small feet were pattering, wooden shoes clattering,
Little hands clapping and little tongues chattering,
And, like fowls in a farm-yard when barley is scattering,
Out came the children running.
All the little boys and girls,
With rosy cheeks and flaxen curls,
And sparkling eyes and teeth like pearls,
Tripping and skipping, ran merrily after
The wonderful music with shouting and laughter.

XIII   The Mayor was dumb, and the Council stood
As if they were changed into blocks of wood,
Unable to move a step, or cry
To the children merrily skipping by—
And could only follow with the eye
That joyous crowd at the Piper's back.
But how the Mayor was on the rack,
And the wretched Council's bosoms beat,
As the Piper turned from the High Street
To where the Weser rolled its waters

---

[1] Dutch coin of very little value.

Right in the way of their sons and daughters!
However he turned from South to West,
And to Koppelberg Hill his steps addressed,
And after him the children pressed;
Great was the joy in every breast.
'He never can cross that mighty top!
He's forced to let the piping drop,
And we shall see our children stop!'
When, lo, as they reached the mountain's side,
A wondrous portal opened wide,
As if a cavern was suddenly hollowed;
And the Piper advanced and the children followed,
And when all were in to the very last,
The door in the mountain-side shut fast.
Did I say, all? No! One was lame,
And could not dance the whole of the way;
And in after years, if you would blame
His sadness, he was used to say,—
'It's dull in our town since my playmates left!
I can't forget that I'm bereft
Of all the pleasant sights they see,
Which the Piper also promised me.
For he led us, he said, to a joyous land,
Joining the town and just at hand,
Where waters gushed and fruit-trees grew,
And flowers put forth a fairer hue,
And everything was strange and new;
The sparrows were brighter than peacocks here,
And their dogs outran our fallow deer,
And honey-bees had lost their stings,
And horses were born with eagles' wings:
And just as I became assured
My lame foot would be speedily cured,
The music stopped and I stood still,
And found myself outside the Hill,
Left alone against my will,
To go now limping as before,
And never hear of that country more!'

XIV   Alas, alas for Hamelin!
        There came into many a burgher's pate

A text which says, that Heaven's Gate
Opes to the Rich at as easy rate
As the needle's eye takes a camel in!
The Mayor sent East, West, North and South,
To offer the Piper, by word of mouth,
    Wherever it was men's lot to find him,
Silver and gold to his heart's content,
If he'd only return the way he went,
    And bring the children behind him.
But when they saw 't was a lost endeavour,
And Piper and dancers were gone for ever,
They made a decree that lawyers never
    Should think their records dated duly
If, after the day of the month and year,
These words did not as well appear,
'And so long after what happened here
    On the Twenty-second of Júly,
Thirteen hundred and seventy-six:'
And the better in memory to fix
The place of the children's last retreat,
They called it, the Pied Piper's Street—
Where any one playing on pipe or tabor
Was sure for the future to lose his labour.
Nor suffered they hostelry or tavern
    To shock with mirth a street so solemn;
But opposite the place of the cavern
    They wrote the story on a column,
And on the great Church-Window painted
The same, to make the world acquainted
How their children were stolen away;
And there it stands to this very day.
And I must not omit to say
That in Transylvania there's a tribe
Of alien people that ascribe
The outlandish ways and dress
On which their neighbours lay such stress,
To their fathers and mothers having risen
Out of some subterraneous prison
Into which they were trepanned[1]

---

[1] Lured.

Long time ago in a mighty band
Out of Hamelin town in Brunswick land,
But how or why, they don't understand.

XV   So, Willy, let me and you be wipers
Of scores out with all men—especially pipers:
And, whether they pipe us free, from rats or fróm mice,
If we've promised them aught, let us keep our promise.

"How They Brought the Good News from Ghent to Aix"

[16—]

I   I sprang to the stirrup, and Joris, and he;
I galloped, Dirck galloped, we galloped all three;
"Good speed!" cried the watch, as the gate-bolts undrew;
"Speed!" echoed the wall to us galloping through;
Behind shut the postern, the lights sank to rest,
And into the midnight we galloped abreast.

II   Not a word to each other; we kept the great pace
Neck by neck, stride by stride, never changing our place;
I turned in my saddle and made its girths tight,
Then shortened each stirrup, and set the pique right,
Rebuckled the cheek-strap, chained slacker the bit,
Nor galloped less steadily Roland a whit.

III   'T was moonset at starting; but while we drew near
Lokeren, the cocks crew and twilight dawned clear;
At Boom, a great yellow star came out to see;
At Düffeld, 't was morning as plain as could be;
And from Mecheln church-steeple we heard the half-chime,
So, Joris broke silence with, "Yet there is time!"

IV   At Aershot, up leaped of a sudden the sun,
And against him the cattle stood black every one,

To stare thro' the mist at us galloping past,
And I saw my stout galloper Roland at last,
With resolute shoulders, each butting away
The haze, as some bluff river headland its spray:

V   And his low head and crest, just one sharp ear bent back
For my voice, and the other pricked out on his track;
And one eye's black intelligence,—ever that glance
O'er its white edge at me, his own master, askance!
And the thick heavy spume-flakes which aye and anon
His fierce lips shook upwards in galloping on.

VI   By Hasselt, Dirck groaned; and cried Joris "Stay spur!
Your Roos galloped bravely, the fault's not in her,
We'll remember at Aix"—for one heard the quick wheeze
Of her chest, saw the stretched neck and staggering knees,
And sunk tail, and horrible heave of the flank,
As down on her haunches she shuddered and sank.

VII   So, we were left galloping, Joris and I,
Past Looz and past Tongres, no cloud in the sky;
The broad sun above laughed a pitiless laugh,
'Neath our feet broke the brittle bright stubble like chaff;
Till over by Dalhem a dome-spire sprang white,
And "Gallop," gasped Joris, "for Aix is in sight!"

VIII   "How they'll greet us!"—and all in a moment his roan
Rolled neck and croup over, lay dead as a stone;
And there was my Roland to bear the whole weight
Of the news which alone could save Aix from her fate,
With his nostrils like pits full of blood to the brim,
And with circles of red for his eye-sockets' rim.

IX   Then I cast loose my buff-coat, each holster let fall,
Shook off both my jack-boots, let go belt and all,
Stood up in the stirrup, leaned, patted his ear,
Called my Roland his pet-name, my horse without peer;
Clapped my hands, laughed and sang, any noise, bad or
        good,
Till at length into Aix Roland galloped and stood.

x   And all I remember is,—friends flocking round
    As I sat with his head 'twixt my knees on the ground;
    And no voice but was praising this Roland of mine,
    As I poured down his throat our last measure of wine,
    Which (the burgesses voted by common consent)
    Was no more than his due who brought good news from
       Ghent.

The Lost Leader

I   Just for a handful of silver he[1] left us,
    Just for a riband to stick in his coat—
Found the one gift of which fortune bereft us,
    Lost all the others, she lets us devote;
They, with the gold to give, doled him out silver,
    So much was theirs who so little allowed:
How all our copper had gone for his service!
    Rags—were they purple, his heart had been proud!
We that had loved him so, followed him, honoured him,
    Lived in his mild and magnificent eye,
Learned his great language, caught his clear accents,
    Made him our pattern to live and to die!
Shakespeare was of us, Milton was for us,
    Burns, Shelley, were with us,—they watch from their graves!
He alone breaks from the van and the freemen,
    He alone sinks to the rear and the slaves!

II   We shall march prospering,—not thro' his presence;
    Songs may inspirit us,—not from his lyre;
Deeds will be done,—while he boasts his quiescence,
    Still bidding crouch whom the rest bade aspire:
Blot out his name, then, record one lost soul more,
    One task more declined, one more footpath untrod,
One more devil's-triumph and sorrow for angels,
    One wrong more to man, one more insult to God!

---

[1] William Wordsworth, who, a political radical in his early years, became increasingly conservative and was named Poet Laureate in 1843.

Life's night begins: let him never come back to us!
  There would be doubt, hesitation and pain,
Forced praise on our part—the glimmer of twilight,
  Never glad confident morning again!
Best fight on well, for we taught him—strike gallantly,
  Menace our heart ere we master his own;
Then let him receive the new knowledge and wait us,
  Pardoned in heaven, the first by the throne!

Home-Thoughts from Abroad

I   Oh, to be in England now that April's there,
    And whoever wakes in England sees, some morning, unaware,
    That the lowest boughs and the brushwood sheaf
    Round the elm-tree bole are in tiny leaf,
    While the chaffinch sings on the orchard bough
    In England—now!

II And after April, when May follows
    And the white-throat builds, and all the swallows!
    Hark, where my blossomed pear-tree in the hedge
    Leans to the field and scatters on the clover
    Blossoms and dewdrops—at the bent spray's edge—
    That's the wise thrush: he sings each song twice over
    Lest you should think he never could recapture
    The first fine careless rapture!
    And, tho' the fields look rough with hoary dew,
    All will be gay when noontide wakes anew
    The buttercups, the little children's dower
    —Far brighter than this gaudy melon-flower!

The Bishop Orders His Tomb at Saint Praxed's Church

ROME, 15—

Vanity, saith the preacher, vanity!
Draw round my bed: is Anselm keeping back?
Nephews—sons mine . . . ah God, I know not! Well—
She, men would have to be your mother once,
Old Gandolf envied me, so fair she was!
What's done is done, and she is dead beside,
Dead long ago, and I am Bishop since,
And as she died so must we die ourselves,
And thence ye may perceive the world's a dream.
Life, how and what is it? As here I lie
In this state-chamber, dying by degrees,
Hours and long hours in the dead night, I ask
"Do I live, am I dead?" Peace, peace seems all.
Saint Praxed's ever was the church for peace;
And so, about this tomb of mine. I fought
With tooth and nail to save my niche, ye know:
—Old Gandolf cozened me, despite my care;
Shrewd was that snatch from out the corner South
He graced his carrion with, God curse the same!
Yet still my niche is not so cramped but thence
One sees the pulpit o' the epistle-side,
And somewhat of the choir, those silent seats,
And up into the aery dome where live
The angels, and a sunbeam's sure to lurk:
And I shall fill my slab of basalt there,
And 'neath my tabernacle take my rest,
With those nine columns round me, two and two,
The odd one at my feet where Anselm stands:
Peach-blossom marble all, the rare, the ripe
As fresh-poured red wine of a mighty pulse.
—Old Gandolf with his paltry onion-stone,[1]
Put me where I may look at him! True peach,

---

[1] Poor quality marble.

Rosy and flawless: how I earned the prize!
Draw close: that conflagration of my church
—What then? So much was saved if aught were missed!
My sons, ye would not be my death? Go dig
The white-grape vineyard where the oil-press stood,
Drop water gently till the surface sink,
And if ye find . . . Ah God, I know not, I! . . .
Bedded in store of rotten fig-leaves soft,
And corded up in a tight olive-frail,[1]
Some lump, ah God, of *lapis lazuli*,
Big as a Jew's head cut off at the nape,
Blue as a vein o'er the Madonna's breast . . .
Sons, all have I bequeathed you, villas, all,
That brave Frascati villa with its bath,
So, let the blue lump poise between my knees,
Like God the Father's globe on both his hands
Ye worship in the Jesu Church so gay,
For Gandolf shall not choose but see and burst!
Swift as a weaver's shuttle fleet our years:
Man goeth to the grave, and where is he?
Did I say, basalt for my slab, sons? Black—
'T was ever antique-black I meant! How else
Shall ye contrast my frieze to come beneath?
The bas-relief in bronze ye promised me,
Those Pans and Nymphs ye wot of, and perchance
Some tripod, thyrsus, with a vase or so,
The Saviour at his sermon on the mount,
Saint Praxed in a glory,[2] and one Pan
Ready to twitch the Nymph's last garment off,
And Moses with the tables . . . but I know
Ye mark me not! What do they whisper thee,
Child of my bowels, Anselm? Ah, ye hope
To revel down my villas while I gasp
Bricked o'er with beggar's mouldy travertine[3]
Which Gandolf from his tomb-top chuckles at!
Nay, boys, ye love me—all of jasper, then!
'T is jasper ye stand pledged to, lest I grieve

---

[1] Olive basket.
[2] Halo.
[3] A white stone.

My bath must needs be left behind, alas!
One block, pure green as a pistachio-nut,
There's plenty jasper somewhere in the world—
And have I not Saint Praxed's ear to pray
Horses for ye, and brown Greek manuscripts,
And mistresses with great smooth marbly limbs?
—That's if ye carve my epitaph aright,
Choice Latin, picked phrase, Tully's every word,
No gaudy ware like Gandolf's second line—
Tully, my masters? Ulpian[1] serves his need!
And then how I shall lie thro' centuries,
And hear the blessed mutter of the mass,
And see God made and eaten all day long,
And feel the steady candle-flame, and taste
Good strong thick stupefying incense-smoke!
For as I lie here, hours of the dead night,
Dying in state and by such slow degrees,
I fold my arms as if they clasped a crook,
And stretch my feet forth straight as stone can point,
And let the bedclothes, for a mortcloth,[2] drop
Into great laps and folds of sculptor's-work:
And as yon tapers dwindle, and strange thoughts
Grow, with a certain humming in my ears,
About the life before I lived this life,
And this life too, popes, cardinals and priests,
Saint Praxed at his sermon on the mount,
Your tall pale mother with her talking eyes,
And new-found agate urns as fresh as day,
And marble's language, Latin pure, discreet,
—Aha, ELUCESCEBAT[3] quoth our friend?
No Tully, said I, Ulpian at the best!
Evil and brief hath been my pilgrimage.
All *lapis*, all, sons! Else I give the Pope
My villas! Will ye ever eat my heart?
Ever your eyes were as a lizard's quick,
They glitter like your mother's for my soul,
Or ye would heighten my impoverished frieze.
Piece out its starved design, and fill my vase

[1] Third-century writer, hardly comparable to Tully (Cicero).
[2] Pall.
[3] "He was illustrious."

With grapes, and add a vizor and a Term.
And to the tripod ye would tie a lynx
That in his struggle throws the thyrsus down,
To comfort me on my entablature[1]
Whereon I am to lie till I must ask
"Do I live, am I dead?" There, leave me, there!
For ye have stabbed me with ingratitude
To death—ye wish it—God, ye wish it! Stone—
Gritstone,[2] a-crumble! Clammy squares which sweat
As if the corpse they keep were oozing through—
And no more *lapis* to delight the world!
Well, go! I bless ye. Fewer tapers there,
But in a row: and, going, turn your backs
—Ay, like departing altar-ministrants,
And leave me in my church, the church for peace
That I may watch at leisure if he leers—
Old Gandolf at me, from his onion-stone,
As still he envied me, so fair she was!

Earth's Immortalities

FAME

See, as the prettiest graves will do in time,
Our poet's wants the freshness of its prime;
Spite of the sexton's browsing horse, the sods
Have struggled through its binding osier rods;
Headstone and half-sunk footstone lean awry,
Wanting the brick-work promised by-and-by;
How the minute gray lichens, plate o'er plate,
Have softened down the crisp-cut name and date!

LOVE

So, the year's done with!
    (*Love me for ever!*)
All March begun with,

---

[1] The word should be "entablement" (a platform for a statue).
[2] Sandstone.

April's endeavour;
May-wreaths that bound me
    June needs must sever;
Now snows fall round me,
    Quenching June's fever—
    (*Love me for ever!*)

Meeting at Night

I   The gray sea and the long black land;
    And the yellow half-moon large and low;
    And the startled little waves that leap
    In fiery ringlets from their sleep,
    As I gain the cove with pushing prow,
    And quench its speed i' the slushy sand.

II   Then a mile of warm sea-scented beach;
    Three fields to cross till a farm appears;
    A tap at the pane, the quick sharp scratch
    And blue spurt of a lighted match,
    And a voice less loud, thro' its joys and fears,
    Than the two hearts beating each to each!

Parting at Morning

Round the cape of a sudden came the sea,
And the sun looked over the mountain's rim:
And straight was a path of gold for him,
And the need of a world of men for me.

Love Among the Ruins

I   Where the quiet-coloured end of evening smiles,
        Miles and miles
  On the solitary pastures where our sheep
        Half-asleep
  Tinkle homeward thro' the twilight, stray or stop
        As they crop—
  Was the site once of a city great and gay,
        (So they say)
  Of our country's very capital, its prince
        Ages since
  Held his court in, gathered councils, wielding far
        Peace or war.

II Now,—the country does not even boast a tree,
        As you see,
  To distinguish slopes of verdure, certain rills
        From the hills
  Intersect and give a name to, (else they run
        Into one)
  Where the domed and daring palace shot its spires
        Up like fires
  O'er the hundred-gated circuit of a wall
        Bounding all,
  Made of marble, men might march on nor be pressed,
        Twelve abreast.

III And such plenty and perfection, see, of grass
        Never was!
  Such a carpet as, this summer-time, o'erspreads
        And embeds
  Every vestige of the city, guessed alone,
        Stock or stone—
  Where a multitude of men breathed joy and woe
        Long ago;
  Lust of glory pricked their hearts up, dread of shame
        Struck them tame;
  And that glory and that shame alike, the gold
        Bought and sold.

IV   Now,—the single little turret that remains
         On the plains,
By the caper overrooted, by the gourd
         Overscored,
While the patching houseleek's head of blossom winks
         Thro' the chinks—
Marks the basement whence a tower in ancient time
         Sprang sublime,
And a burning ring, all round, the chariots traced
         As they raced,
And the monarch and his minions and his dames
         Viewed the games.

V   And I know—while thus the quiet-coloured eve
         Smiles to leave
To their folding, all our many tinkling fleece
         In such peace,
And the slopes and rills in undistinguished gray
         Melt away—
That a girl with eager eyes and yellow hair
         Waits me there
In the turret whence the charioteers caught soul
         For the goal,
When the king looked, where she looks now, breathless, dumb
         Till I come.

VI   But he looked upon the city, every side,
         Far and wide,
All the mountains topped with temples, all the glades'
         Colonnades,
All the causeys, bridges, aqueducts,—and then,
         All the men!
When I do come, she will speak not, she will stand,
         Either hand
On my shoulder, give her eyes the first embrace
         Of my face,
Ere we rush, ere we extinguish sight and speech
         Each on each.

VII   In one year they sent a million fighters forth
         South and North,
And they built their gods a brazen pillar high

As the sky,
Yet reserved a thousand chariots in full force—
    Gold, of course.
Oh heart! oh blood that freezes, blood that burns!
    Earth's returns
For whole centuries of folly, noise and sin!
    Shut them in,
With their triumphs and their glories and the rest!
    Love is best.

A Lovers' Quarrel

I   Oh, what a dawn of day!
    How the March sun feels like May!
        All is blue again
        After last night's rain,
    And the South dries the hawthorn-spray.
        Only, my Love's away!
    I'd as lief that the blue were gray.

II   Runnels, which rillets swell,
    Must be dancing down the dell,
        With a foaming head
        On the beryl bed
    Paven smooth as a hermit's cell:
        Each with a tale to tell,
    Could my Love but attend as well.

III   Dearest, three months ago!
    When we lived blocked-up with snow,—
        When the wind would edge
        In and in his wedge,
    In, as far as the point could go—
        Not to our ingle, though,
    Where we loved each the other so!

IV   Laughs with so little cause!
    We devised games out of straws.
        We would try and trace

One another's face
In the ash, as an artist draws;
    Free on each other's flaws,
How we chattered like two church daws!

v What's in the "Times"?—a scold
At the Emperor deep and cold;
    He has taken a bride
    To his gruesome side,
That's as fair as himself is bold:
    There they sit ermine-stoled,
And she powders her hair with gold.

vi Fancy the Pampas' sheen!
Miles and miles of gold and green
    Where the sunflowers blow
    In a solid glow,
And—to break now and then the screen—
    Black neck and eyeballs keen,
Up a wild horse leaps between!

vii Try, will our table turn?
Lay your hands there light, and yearn
    Till the yearning slips
    Thro' the finger-tips
In a fire which a few discern,
    And a very few feel burn,
And the rest, they may live and learn!

viii Then we would up and pace,
For a change, about the place,
    Each with arm o'er neck:
    'T is our quarter-deck,
We are seamen in woeful case.
    Help in the ocean-space!
Or, if no help, we'll embrace.

ix See, how she looks now, dressed
In a sledging-cap and vest!
    'T is a huge fur cloak—
    Like a reindeer's yoke

Falls the lappet along the breast:
        Sleeves for her arms to rest,
Or to hang, as my Love likes best.

x Teach me to flirt a fan
As the Spanish ladies can,
        Or I tint your lip
        With a burnt stick's tip
And you turn into such a man!
        Just the two spots that span
Half the bill of the young male swan.

XI Dearest, three months ago,
When the mesmerizer Snow
        With his hand's first sweep
        Put the earth to sleep,
'T was a time when the heart could show
        All—how was earth to know,
Neath the mute hand's to-and-fro?

XII Dearest, three months ago,
When we loved each other so,
        Lived and loved the same
        Till an evening came
When a shaft from the devil's bow
        Pierced to our ingle-glow,
And the friends were friend and foe!

XIII Not from the heart beneath—
'T was a bubble born of breath,
        Neither sneer nor vaunt,
        Nor reproach nor taunt.
See a word, how it severeth!
        Oh, power of life and death
In the tongue, as the Preacher saith!

XIV Woman, and will you cast
For a word, quite off at last
        Me, your own, your You,—
        Since, as truth is true,
I was You all the happy past—

Me do you leave aghast
With the memories We amassed?

xv   Love, if you knew the light
That your soul casts in my sight,
        How I look to you
        For the pure and true,
And the beauteous and the right,—
        Bear with a moment's spite
When a mere mote threats the white!

xvi   What of a hasty word?
Is the fleshly heart not stirred
        By a worm's pin-prick
        Where its roots are quick?
See the eye, by a fly's foot blurred—
        Ear, when a straw is heard
Scratch the brain's coat of curd!

xvii   Foul be the world or fair
More or less, how can I care?
        'T is the world the same
        For my praise or blame,
And endurance is easy there.
        Wrong in the one thing rare—
Oh, it is hard to bear!

xviii   Here's the spring back or close,
When the almond-blossom blows;
        We shall have the word
        In a minor third
There is none but the cuckoo knows:
        Heaps of the guelder-rose!
I must bear with it, I suppose.

xix   Could but November come,
Were the noisy birds struck dumb
        At the warning slash
        Of his driver's-lash—
I would laugh like the valiant Thumb
        Facing the castle glum
And the giant's fee-faw-fum!

xx   Then, were the world well-stripped
     Of the gear wherein equipped
          We can stand apart,
          Heart dispense with heart
     In the sun, with the flowers unnipped,—
          Oh, the world's hangings ripped,
     We were both in a bare-walled crypt!

xxi Each in the crypt would cry
     "But one freezes here! and why?
          When a heart, as chill,
          At my own would thrill
     Back to life, and its fires out-fly?
          Heart, shall we live or die?
     The rest . . . settle by-and-by!"

xxii So, she'd efface the score,
     And forgive me as before.
          It is twelve o'clock:
          I shall hear her knock
     In the worst of a storm's uproar:
          I shall pull her through the door,
     I shall have her for evermore!

Up at a Villa—Down in the City

(AS DISTINGUISHED BY AN ITALIAN PERSON OF QUALITY)

i   Had I but plenty of money, money enough and to spare,
     The house for me, no doubt, were a house in the city-square;
     Ah, such a life, such a life, as one leads at the window there!

ii   Something to see, by Bacchus, something to hear, at least!
     There, the whole day long, one's life is a perfect feast;
     While up at a villa one lives, I maintain it, no more than a
          beast.

iii Well now, look at our villa! stuck like the horn of a bull
     Just on a mountain edge as bare as the creature's skull,

Save a mere shag of a bush with hardly a leaf to pull!
—I scratch my own, sometimes, to see if the hair's turned
wool.

IV   But the city, oh the city—the square with the houses! Why?
They are stone-faced, white as a curd, there's something to
take the eye!
Houses in four straight lines, not a single front awry;
You watch who crosses and gossips, who saunters, who hur-
ries by;
Green blinds, as a matter of course, to draw when the sun gets
high;
And the shops with fanciful signs which are painted properly.

V   What of a villa? Tho' winter be over in March by rights,
'T is May perhaps ere the snow shall have withered well off the
heights:
You've the brown ploughed land before, where the oxen steam
and wheeze,
And the hills over-smoked behind by the faint gray olive-trees.

VI   Is it better in May, I ask you? You've summer all at once;
In a day he leaps complete with a few strong April suns.
'Mid the sharp short emerald wheat, scarce risen three fingers
well,
The wild tulip, at end of its tube, blows out its great red bell
Like a thin clear bubble of blood, for the children to pick and
sell.

VII   Is it ever hot in the square? There's a fountain to spout and
splash!
In the shade it sings and springs; in the shine such foam-bows
flash
On the horses with curling fish-tails, that prance and paddle
and pash
Round the lady atop in her conch—fifty gazers do not abash,
Tho' all that she wears is some weeds round her waist in a sort
of sash.

VIII   All the year long at the villa, nothing to see though you linger,
Except yon cypress that points like death's lean lifted fore-
finger.

Some think fireflies pretty, when they mix i' the corn and
    mingle,
Or thrid the stinking hemp till the stalks of it seem a-tingle.
Late August or early September, the stunning cicala is shrill,
And the bees keep their tiresome whine round the resinous firs
    on the hill.
Enough of the seasons,—I spare you the months of the fever
    and chill.

IX   Ere you open your eyes in the city, the blessed church-bells
    begin:
No sooner the bells leave off than the diligence rattles in:
You get the pick of the news, and it costs you never a pin.
By and by there's the traveling doctor gives pills, lets blood,
    draws teeth;
Or the Pulcinello-trumpet breaks up the market beneath.
At the post-office such a scene-picture—the new play, piping
    hot!
And a notice how, only this morning, three liberal thieves
    were shot.
Above it, behold the Archbishop's most fatherly of rebukes,
And beneath, with his crown and his lion, some little new law
    of the Duke's!
Or a sonnet with flowery marge, to the Reverend Don So-
    and-so
Who is Dante, Boccaccio, Petrarca, St. Jerome and Cicero,
"And moreover," (the sonnet goes rhyming,) "the skirts of St.
    Paul has reached,
Having preached us those six Lent-lectures more unctuous
    than ever he preached."
Noon strikes,—here sweeps the procession! our Lady borne
    smiling and smart,
With a pink gauze gown all spangles, and seven swords stuck
    in her heart!
Bang-whang-whang goes the drum, *tootle-te-tootle* the
    fife;
No keeping one's haunches still: it's the greatest pleasure in
    life.

X   But bless you, it's dear—it's dear! fowls, wine, at double the
    rate.

They have clapped a new tax upon salt, and what oil pays
    passing the gate
It's a horror to think of. And so, the villa for me, not the city!
Beggars can scarcely be choosers: but still—ah, the pity, the
    pity!
Look, two and two go the priests, then the monks with cowls
    and sandals,
And the penitents dressed in white shirts, a-holding the yel-
    low candles;
One, he carries a flag up straight, and another a cross with
    handles,
And the Duke's guard brings up the rear, for the better preven-
    tion of scandals:
Bang-whang-whang goes the drum, *tootle-te-tootle* the fife.
Oh, a day in the city-square, there is no such pleasure in life!

Fra Lippo Lippi[1]

I am poor brother Lippo, by your leave!
You need not clap your torches to my face.
Zooks, what's to blame? you think you see a monk!
What, 't is past midnight, and you go the rounds,
And here you catch me at an alley's end
Where sportive ladies leave their doors ajar?
The Carmine's my cloister: hunt it up,
Do,—harry out, if you must show your zeal,
Whatever rat, there, haps on his wrong hole,
And nip each softling of a wee white mouse,
Weke, weke, that's crept to keep him company!
Aha, you know your betters? Then, you'll take
Your hand away that's fiddling on my throat,
And please to know me likewise. Who am I?
Why, one, sir, who is lodging with a friend
Three streets off—he's a certain . . . how d' ye call?
Master—a . . . Cosimo of the Medici,
I' the house that caps the corner. Boh! you were best!
Remember and tell me, the day you're hanged,
How you affected such a gullet's-gripe!

---

[1] A fifteenth-century Florentine painter, pupil of Masaccio (Tommaso Guidi).

But you, sir, it concerns you that your knaves
Pick up a manner nor discredit you:
Zooks, are we pilchards, that they sweep the streets
And count fair prize what comes into their net?
He's Judas to a tittle, that man is!
Just such a face! Why, sir, you make amends.
Lord, I'm not angry! Bid your hangdogs go
Drink out this quarter-florin to the health
Of the munificent House that harbours me
(And many more besides, lads! more beside!)
And all's come square again. I'd like his face—
His, elbowing on his comrade in the door
With the pike and lantern,—for the slave that holds
John Baptist's head a-dangle by the hair
With one hand ("Look you, now," as who should say)
And his weapon in the other, yet unwiped!
It's not your chance to have a bit of chalk,
A wood-coal or the like? or you should see!
Yes, I'm the painter, since you style me so.
What, brother Lippo's doings, up and down,
You know them, and they take you? like enough!
I saw the proper twinkle in your eye—
'Tell you, I liked your looks at very first.
Let's sit and set things straight now, hip to haunch.
Here's spring come, and the nights one makes up bands
To roam the town and sing out carnival,
And I've been three weeks shut within my mew,
A-painting for the great man, saints and saints
And saints again. I could not paint all night—
Ouf! I leaned out of window for fresh air.
There came a hurry of feet and little feet,
A sweep of lute-strings, laughs, and whifts of song,
Flower o' the broom,
Take away love, and our earth is a tomb!
Flower o' the quince,
I let Lisa go, and what good in life since?
Flower o' the thyme—and so on. Round they went.
Scarce had they turned the corner when a titter
Like the skipping of rabbits by moonlight,—three slim shapes,
And a face that looked up . . . zooks, sir, flesh and blood,
That's all I'm made of! Into shreds it went,

Curtain and counterpane and coverlet,
All the bed-furniture—a dozen knots,
There was a ladder! Down I let myself,
Hands and feet, scrambling somehow, and so dropped,
And after them. I came up with the fun
Hard by Saint Laurence, hail fellow, well met,—
Flower o' the rose,
If I've been merry, what matter who knows?
And so, as I was stealing back again,
To get to bed and have a bit of sleep
Ere I rise up to-morrow and go work
On Jerome knocking at his poor old breast
With his great round stone to subdue the flesh,
You snap me of the sudden. Ah, I see!
Tho' your eye twinkles still, you shake your head—
Mine's shaved—a monk, you say—the sting's in that!
If Master Cosimo announced himself,
Mum's the word naturally; but a monk!
Come, what am I a beast for? tell us, now!
I was a baby when my mother died
And father died and left me in the street.
I starved there, God knows how, a year or two
On fig-skins, melon-parings, rinds and shucks,
Refuse and rubbish. One fine frosty day,
My stomach being empty as your hat,
The wind doubled me up and down I went.
Old Aunt Lapaccia trussed me with one hand,
(Its fellow was a stinger as I knew)
And so along the wall, over the bridge,
By the straight cut to the convent. Six words there,
While I stood munching my first bread that month:
"So, boy, you're minded," quoth the good fat father
Wiping his own mouth, 't was refection-time,—
"To quit this very miserable world?
Will you renounce" . . . "the mouthful of bread?" thought I;
By no means! Brief, they made a monk of me;
I did renounce the world, its pride and greed,
Palace, farm, villa, shop and banking-house,
Trash, such as these poor devils of Medici
Have given their hearts to—all at eight years old.
Well, sir, I found in time, you may be sure,

'T was not for nothing—the good bellyful,
The warm serge and the rope that goes all round,
And day-long blessed idleness beside!
"Let's see what the urchin's fit for"—that came next.
Not overmuch their way, I must confess.
Such a to-do! They tried me with their books:
Lord, they'd have taught me Latin in pure waste!
Flower o' the clove,
All the Latin I construe is, "amo" I love!
But, mind you, when a boy starves in the streets
Eight years together, as my fortune was,
Watching folk's faces to know who will fling
The bit of half-stripped grape-bunch he desires,
And who will curse or kick him for his pains,—
Which gentleman processional and fine,
Holding a candle to the Sacrament,
Will wink and let him lift a plate and catch
The droppings of the wax to sell again,
Or holla for the Eight[1] and have him whipped,—
How say I?—nay, which dog bites, which lets drop
His bone from the heap of offal in the street,—
Why, soul and sense of him grow sharp alike,
He learns the look of things, and none the less
For admonition from the hunger-pinch.
I had a store of such remarks, be sure,
Which, after I found leisure, turned to use:
I drew men's faces on my copy-books,
Scrawled them within the antiphonary's[2] marge,
Joined legs and arms to the long music-notes,
Found eyes and nose and chin for A's and B's
And made a string of pictures of the world
Betwixt the ins and outs of verb and noun,
On the wall, the bench, the door. The monks looked black.
"Nay," quoth the Prior, "turn him out, d' ye say?
In no wise. Lose a crow and catch a lark.
What if at last we get our man of parts,
We Carmelites, like those Camaldolese
And Preaching Friars, to do our church up fine

---

[1] The magistrates of Florence.
[2] Book of choral music.

And put the front on it that ought to be!"
And hereupon he bade me daub away.
Thank you! my head being crammed, the walls a blank,
Never was such prompt disemburdening.
First every sort of monk, the black and white,
I drew them, fat and lean: then, folk at church,
From good old gossips waiting to confess
Their cribs of barrel-droppings, candle-ends,—
To the breathless fellow at the altar-foot,
Fresh from his murder, safe and sitting there
With the little children round him in a row
Of admiration, half for his beard, and half
For that white anger of his victim's son
Shaking a fist at him with one fierce arm,
Signing himself with the other because of Christ
(Whose sad face on the cross sees only this
After the passion of a thousand years)
Till some poor girl, her apron o'er her head,
(Which the intense eyes looked through) came at eve
On tiptoe, said a word, dropped in a loaf,
Her pair of ear-rings and a bunch of flowers
(The brute took growling) prayed, and so was gone.
I painted all, then cried, " 'T is ask and have;
Choose, for more's ready!"—laid the ladder flat,
And showed my covered bit of cloister-wall.
The monks closed in a circle and praised loud
Till checked, taught what to see and not to see,
Being simple bodies,—"That's the very man!
Look at the boy who stoops to pat the dog!
That woman's like the Prior's niece who comes
To care about his asthma: it's the life!"
But there my triumph's straw-fire flared and funked;
Their betters took their turn to see and say:
The Prior and the learned pulled a face
And stopped all that in no time. "How! what's here?
Quite from the mark of painting, bless us all!
Faces, arms, legs and bodies like the true
As much as pea and pea! it's devil's game!
Your business is not to catch men with show,
With homage to the perishable clay,
But lift them over it, ignore it all,

Make them forget there's such a thing as flesh.
Your business is to paint the souls of men—
Man's soul, and it's a fire, smoke . . no, it's not . .
It's vapour done up like a new-born babe—
(In that shape when you die it leaves your mouth)
It's . . well, what matters talking, it's the soul!
Give us no more of body than shows soul!
Here's Giotto, with his Saint a-praising God,
That sets us praising,—why not stop with him?
Why put all thoughts of praise out of our head
With wonder at lines, colours, and what not?
Paint the soul, never mind the legs and arms!
Rub all out, try at it a second time!
Oh, that white smallish female with the breasts,
She's just my niece . . . Herodias, I would say,—
Who went and danced, and got men's heads cut off!
Have it all out!" Now, is this sense, I ask?
A fine way to paint soul, by painting body
So ill, the eye can't stop there, must go further
And can't fare worse! Thus, yellow does for white
When what you put for yellow's simply black,
And any sort of meaning looks intense
When all beside itself means and looks naught.
Why can't a painter lift each foot in turn,
Left foot and right foot, go a double step,
Make his flesh liker and his soul more like,
Both in their order? Take the prettiest face,
The Prior's niece . . . patron-saint—is it so pretty
You can't discover if it means hope, fear,
Sorrow or joy? won't beauty go with these?
Suppose I've made her eyes all right and blue,
Can't I take breath and try to add life's flash,
And then add soul and heighten them threefold?
Or say there's beauty with no soul at all—
(I never saw it—put the case the same—)
If you get simple beauty and naught else,
You get about the best thing God invents:
That's somewhat: and you'll find the soul you have missed,
Within yourself, when you return him thanks.
"Rub all out!" Well, well, there's my life, in short,
And so the thing has gone on ever since.

I'm grown a man no doubt, I've broken bounds:
You should not take a fellow eight years old
And make him swear to never kiss the girls.
I'm my own master, paint now as I please—
Having a friend, you see, in the Corner-house!
Lord, it's fast holding by the rings in front—
Those great rings serve more purposes than just
To plant a flag in, or tie up a horse!
And yet the old schooling sticks, the old grave eyes
Are peeping o'er my shoulder as I work,
The heads shake still—"It's art's decline, my son!
You're not of the true painters, great and old;
Brother Angelico's the man, you'll find;
Brother Lorenzo stands his single peer:
Fag on at flesh, you'll never make the third!"
Flower o' the pine,
You keep your mistr . . . manners, and I'll stick to mine!
I'm not the third, then: bless us, they must know!
Don't you think they're the likeliest to know,
They with their Latin? So, I swallow my rage,
Clench my teeth, suck my lips in tight, and paint
To please them—sometimes do, and sometimes don't;
For, doing most, there's pretty sure to come
A turn, some warm eve finds me at my saints—
A laugh, a cry, the business of the world—
(*Flower o' the peach,*
Death for us all, and his own life for each!)
And my whole soul revolves, the cup runs over,
The world and life's too big to pass for a dream,
And I do these wild things in sheer despite,
And play the fooleries you catch me at,
In pure rage! The old mill-horse, out at grass
After hard years, throws up his stiff heels so,
Altho' the miller does not preach to him
The only good of grass is to make chaff.
What would men have? Do they like grass or no—
May they or may n't they? all I want's the thing
Settled for ever one way. As it is,
You tell too many lies and hurt yourself:
You don't like what you only like too much,
You do like what, if given you at your word,
You find abundantly detestable.

For me, I think I speak as I was taught:
I always see the garden, and God there
A-making man's wife: and, my lesson learned,
The value and significance of flesh,
I can't unlearn ten minutes afterwards.

    You understand me: I'm a beast, I know.
But see, now—why, I see as certainly
As that the morning-star's about to shine,
What will hap some day. We've a youngster here
Comes to our convent, studies what I do,
Slouches and stares and lets no atom drop:
His name is Guidi—he'll not mind the monks—
They call him Hulking Tom, he lets them talk—
He picks my practice up—he'll paint apace,
I hope so—tho' I never live so long,
I know what's sure to follow. You be judge!
You speak no Latin more than I, belike;
However, you're my man, you've seen the world
—The beauty and the wonder and the power,
The shapes of things, their colours, lights and shades,
Changes, surprises,—and God made it all!
—For what? Do you feel thankful, ay or no,
For this fair town's face, yonder river's line,
The mountain round it and the sky above,
Much more the figures of man, woman, child,
These are the frame to? What's it all about?
To be passed over, despised? or dwelt upon,
Wondered at? oh, this last of course!—you say.
But why not do as well as say,—paint these
Just as they are, careless what comes of it?
God's works—paint any one, and count it crime
To let a truth slip. Don't object, "His works
Are here already; nature is complete:
Suppose you reproduce her—(which you can't)
There's no advantage! you must beat her, then."
For, don't you mark? we're made so that we love
First when we see them painted, things we have passed
Perhaps a hundred times nor cared to see;
And so they are better, painted—better to us,
Which is the same thing. Art was given for that;
God uses us to help each other so,

Lending our minds out. Have you noticed, now,
Your cullion's hanging face? A bit of chalk,
And trust me but you should, though! How much more
If I drew higher things with the same truth!
That were to take the Prior's pulpit-place,
Interpret God to all of you! Oh, oh,
It makes me mad to see what men shall do
And we in our graves! This world's no blot for us
Nor blank; it means intensely, and means good:
To find its meaning is my meat and drink.
"Ay, but you don't so instigate to prayer!"
Strikes in the Prior: "when your meaning's plain
It does not say to folk—remember matins,
Or, mind you fast next Friday!" Why, for this
What need of art at all? A skull and bones,
Two bits of stick nailed cross-wise, or, what's best,
A bell to chime the hour with, does as well.
I painted a Saint Laurence six months since
At Prato, splashed the fresco in fine style:
"How looks my painting, now the scaffold's down?"
I ask a brother: "Hugely," he returns—
"Already not one phiz of your three slaves
Who turn the Deacon off his toasted side,
But's scratched and prodded to our heart's content,
The pious people have so eased their own
With coming to say prayers there in a rage:
We get on fast to see the bricks beneath.
Expect another job this time next year,
For pity and religion grow i' the crowd—
Your painting serves its purpose!" Hang the fools!

—That is—you'll not mistake an idle word
Spoke in a huff by a poor monk, Got wot,
Tasting the air this spicy night which turns
The unaccustomed head like Chianti wine!
Oh, the church knows! don't misreport me, now!
It's natural a poor monk out of bounds
Should have his apt word to excuse himself:
And hearken how I plot to make amends.
I have bethought me: I shall paint a piece
. . . There's for you! Give me six months, then go, see

Something in Sant' Ambrogio's! Bless the nuns!
They want a cast o' my office.[1] I shall paint
God in the midst, Madonna and her babe,
Ringed by a bowery flowery angel-brood,
Lilies and vestments and white faces, sweet
As puff on puff of grated orris-root
When ladies crowd to church at midsummer.
And then i' the front, of course a saint or two—
Saint John, because he saves the Florentines,
Saint Ambrose, who puts down in black and white
The convent's friends and gives them a long day,
And Job, I must have him there past mistake,
The man of Uz (and Us without the z,
Painters who need his patience). Well, all these
Secured at their devotion, up shall come
Out of a corner when you least expect,
As one by a dark stair into a great light,
Music and talking, who but Lippo! I!—
Mazed, motionless and moon-struck—I'm the man!
Back I shrink—what is this I see and hear?
I, caught up with my monk's things by mistake,
My old serge gown and rope that goes all round,
I, in this presence, this pure company!
Where's a hole, where's a corner for escape?
Then steps a sweet angelic slip of a thing
Forward, puts out a soft palm—"Not so fast!"
—Addresses the celestial presence, "nay—
He made you and devised you, after all,
Tho' he's none of you! Could Saint John there, draw—
His camel-hair make up a painting-brush?
We come to brother Lippo for all that,
Iste perfecit opus!"[2] So, all smile—
I shuffle sideways with my blushing face
Under the cover of a hundred wings
Thrown like a spread of kirtles[3] when you're gay
And play hot cockles, all the doors being shut,

[1] Sample of my work.
[2] Understood by Browning to mean "This man did the work." The Latin should read *Is perfecit opus* ("This man arranged the work").
[3] Skirts.

Till, wholly unexpected, in there pops
The hothead husband! Thus I scuttle off
To some safe bench behind, not letting go
The palm of her, the little lily thing
That spoke the good word for me in the nick,
Like the Prior's niece . . . Saint Lucy, I would say.
And so all's saved for me, and for the church
A pretty picture gained. Go, six months hence!
Your hand, sir, and good bye: no lights, no lights!
The street's hushed, and I know my own way back,
Don't fear me! There's the gray beginning. Zooks!

A Toccata of Galuppi's

I   Oh Galuppi, Baldassaro,[1] this is very sad to find!
    I can hardly misconceive you; it would prove me deaf and
       blind;
    But altho' I take your meaning, 't is with such a heavy mind!

II   Here you come with your old music, and here's all the good it
       brings.
    What, they lived once thus at Venice where the merchants
       were the kings,
    Where St. Mark's is, where the Doges used to wed the sea with
       rings?

III   Ay, because the sea's the street there; and 't is arched by . . .
       what you call
    . . . Shylock's bridge with houses on it, where they kept the
       carnival:
    I was never out of England—it's as if I saw it all.

IV   Did young people take their pleasure when the sea was warm
       in May?

---

[1] The Venetian composer Baldassare Galuppi (1706–85).

Balls and masks begun at midnight, burning ever to mid-day,
When they made up fresh adventures for the morrow, do you
    say?

v   Was a lady such a lady, cheeks so round and lips so red,—
On her neck the small face buoyant, like a bell-flower on its
    bed,
O'er the breast's superb abundance where a man might base
    his head?

vi   Well, and it was graceful of them: they'd break talk off and
    afford
—She, to bite her mask's black velvet—he, to finger on his
    sword,
While you sat and played Toccatas, stately at the clavichord?

vii   What? Those lesser thirds so plaintive, sixths diminished,
    sigh on sigh,
Told them something? Those suspensions, those solutions—
    "Must we die?"
Those commiserating sevenths—"Life might last! we can but
    try!"

viii   "Were you happy?"—"Yes."—"And are you still as happy?"—
    "Yes. And you?"
—"Then, more kisses!"—"Did I stop them, when a million
    seemed so few?"
Hark, the dominant's persistence till it must be answered to!

ix   So, an octave struck the answer. Oh, they praised you, I dare
    say!
"Brave Galuppi! that was music! good alike at grave and gay!
I can always leave off talking when I hear a master play!"

x   Then they left you for their pleasure: till in due time, one by
    one,
Some with lives that came to nothing, some with deeds as
    well undone,
Death stepped tacitly and took them where they never see the
    sun.

XI But when I sit down to reason, think to take my stand nor swerve,
While I triumph o'er a secret wrung from nature's close reserve,
In you come with your cold music till I creep thro' every nerve.

XII Yes, you, like a ghostly cricket, creaking where a house was burned:
"Dust and ashes, dead and done with, Venice spent what Venice earned.
The soul, doubtless, is immortal—where a soul can be discerned.

XIII "Yours for instance: you know physics, something of geology,
Mathematics are your pastime; souls shall rise in their degree;
Butterflies may dread extinction,—you'll not die, it can not be!

XIV "As for Venice and her people, merely born to bloom and drop,
Here on earth they bore their fruitage, mirth and folly were the crop:
What of soul was left, I wonder, when the kissing had to stop?

XV "Dust and ashes!" So you creak it, and I want the heart to scold.
Dear dead women, with such hair, too—what's become of all the gold
Used to hang and brush their bosoms? I feel chilly and grown old.

An Epistle Containing the Strange Medical Experience of Karshish, the Arab Physician

Karshish, the picker-up of learning's crumbs,
The not-incurious in God's handiwork

(This man's-flesh he hath admirably made,
Blown like a bubble, kneaded like a paste,
To coop up and keep down on earth a space
That puff of vapour from his mouth, man's soul)
—To Abib, all-sagacious in our art,
Breeder in me of what poor skill I boast,
Like me inquisitive how pricks and cracks
Befall the flesh thro' too much stress and strain,
Whereby the wily vapour fain would slip
Back and rejoin its source before the term,—
And aptest in contrivance (under God)
To baffle it by deftly stopping such:—
The vagrant Scholar to his Sage at home
Sends greeting (health and knowledge, fame with peace)
Three samples of true snake-stone—rarer still,
One of the other sort, the melon-shaped,
(But fitter, pounded fine, for charms than drugs)
And writeth now the twenty-second time.

    My journeyings were brought to Jericho:
Thus I resume. Who studious in our art
Shall count a little labour unrepaid?
I have shed sweat enough, left flesh and bone
On many a flinty furlong of this land.
Also, the country-side is all on fire
With rumours of a marching hitherward:
Some say Vespasian cometh, some, his son.
A black lynx snarled and pricked a tufted ear:
Lust of my blood inflamed his yellow balls:
I cried and threw my staff and he was gone.
Twice have the robbers stripped and beaten me,
And once a town declared me for a spy;
But at the end, I reach Jerusalem,
Since this poor covert where I pass the night,
This Bethany, lies scarce the distance thence
A man with plague-sores at the third degree
Runs till he drops down dead. Thou laughest here!
'Sooth, it elates me, thus reposed and safe,
To void the stuffing of my travel-scrip
And share with thee whatever Jewry yields.
A viscid choler is observable

In tertians,[1] I was nearly bold to say;
And falling-sickness[2] hath a happier cure
Than our school wots of: there's a spider here
Weaves no web, watches on the ledge of tombs,
Sprinkled with mottles on an ash-gray back;
Take five and drop them . . . but who knows his mind,
The Syrian run-a-gate I trust this to?
His service payeth me a sublimate
Blown up his nose to help the ailing eye.
Best wait: I reach Jerusalem at morn,
There set in order my experiences,
Gather what most deserves, and give thee all—
Or I might add, Judæa's gum-tragacanth
Scales off in purer flakes, shines clearer-grained,
Cracks 'twixt the pestle and the porphyry,
In fine exceeds our produce. Scalp-disease
Confounds me, crossing so with leprosy:
Thou hadst admired one sort I gained at Zoar—
But zeal outruns discretion. Here I end.

Yet stay! my Syrian blinketh gratefully,
Protesteth his devotion is my price—
Suppose I write what harms not, tho' he steal?
I half resolve to tell thee, yet I blush,
What set me off a-writing first of all.
An itch I had, a sting to write, a tang!
For, be it this town's barrenness—or else
The Man had something in the look of him—
His case has struck me far more than 't is worth.
So, pardon if—(lest presently I lose,
In the great press of novelty at hand,
The care and pains this somehow stole from me)
I bid thee take the thing while fresh in mind,
Almost in sight—for, wilt thou have the truth?
The very man is gone from me but now,
Whose ailment is the subject of discourse.
Thus then, and let thy better wit help all!

    'T is but a case of mania: subinduced

---

[1] Fevers that recur every other day.
[2] Epilepsy.

By epilepsy, at the turning-point
Of trance prolonged unduly some three days
When, by the exhibition[1] of some drug
Or spell, exorcisation, stroke of art
Unknown to me and which 't were well to know,
The evil thing, out-breaking all at once,
Left the man whole and sound of body indeed,—
But, flinging (so to speak) life's gates too wide,
Making a clear house of it too suddenly,
The first conceit that entered might inscribe
Whatever it was minded on the wall
So plainly at that vantage, as it were,
(First come, first served) that nothing subsequent
Attaineth to erase those fancy-scrawls
The just-returned and new-established soul
Hath gotten now so thoroughly by heart
That henceforth she will read or these or none.
And first—the man's own firm conviction rests
That he was dead (in fact they buried him)
—That he was dead and then restored to life
By a Nazarene physician of his tribe:
—'Sayeth, the same bade "Rise," and he did rise.
"Such cases are diurnal," thou wilt cry.
Not so this figment!—not, that such a fume,
Instead of giving way to time and health,
Should eat itself into the life of life,
As saffron tingeth flesh, blood, bones, and all!
For see, how he takes up the after-life.
The man—it is one Lazarus a Jew,
Sanguine, proportioned, fifty years of age,
The body's habit wholly laudable,
As much, indeed, beyond the common health
As he were made and put aside to show.
Think, could we penetrate by any drug
And bathe the wearied soul and worried flesh,
And bring it clear and fair, by three days' sleep!
Whence has the man the balm that brightens all?
This grown man eyes the world now like a child.
Some elders of his tribe, I should premise,

---

[1]Administration.

Led in their friend, obedient as a sheep,
To bear my inquisition. While they spoke,
Now sharply, now with sorrow,—told the case,—
He listened not except I spoke to him,
But folded his two hands and let them talk,
Watching the flies that buzzed: and yet no fool.
And that's a sample how his years must go.
Look if a beggar, in fixed middle-life,
Should find a treasure,—can he use the same
With straitened habits and with tastes starved small,
And take at once to his impoverished brain
The sudden element that changes things,
That sets the undreamed-of rapture at his hand,
And puts the cheap old joy in the scorned dust?
Is he not such an one as moves to mirth—
Warily parsimonious, when no need,
Wasteful as drunkenness at undue times?
All prudent counsel as to what befits
The golden mean, is lost on such an one:
The man's fantastic will is the man's law.
So here—we call the treasure knowledge, say,
Increased beyond the fleshly faculty—
Heaven opened to a soul while yet on earth,
Earth forced on a soul's use while seeing heaven:
The man is witless of the size, the sum,
The value in proportion of all things,
Or whether it be little or be much.
Discourse to him of prodigious armaments
Assembled to besiege his city now,
And of the passing of a mule with gourds—
'T is one! Then take it on the other side,
Speak of some trifling fact,—he will gaze rapt
With stupor at its very littleness,
(Far as I see) as if in that indeed
He caught prodigious import, whole results;
And so will turn to us the bystanders
In ever the same stupor (note this point)
That we too see not with his opened eyes.
Wonder and doubt come wrongly into play,
Preposterously, at cross purposes.
Should his child sicken unto death,—why, look

For scarce abatement of his cheerfulness,
Or pretermission of the daily craft!
While a word, gesture, glance from that same child
At play or in the school or laid asleep,
Will startle him to an agony of fear,
Exasperation, just as like. Demand
The reason why—" 't is but a word," object—
"A gesture"—he regards thee as our lord
Who lived there in the pyramid alone,
Looked at us (dost thou mind?) when, being young,
We both would unadvisedly recite
Some charm's beginning, from that book of his,
Able to bid the sun throb wide and burst
All into stars, as suns grown old are wont.
Thou and the child have each a veil alike
Thrown o'er your heads, from under which ye both
Stretch your blind hands and trifle with a match
Over a mine of Greek fire, did ye know!
He holds on firmly to some thread of life—
(It is the life to lead perforcedly)
Which runs across some vast distracting orb
Of glory on either side that meagre thread,
Which, conscious of, he must not enter yet—
The spiritual life around the earthly life:
The law of that is known to him as this,
His heart and brain move there, his feet stay here.
So is the man perplext with impulses
Sudden to start off crosswise, not straight on,
Proclaiming what is right and wrong across,
And not along, this black thread thro' the blaze—
"It should be" balked by "here it can not be."
And oft the man's soul springs into his face
As if he saw again and heard again
His sage that bade him "Rise" and he did rise.
Something, a word, a tick o' the blood within
Admonishes: then back he sinks at once
To ashes, who was very fire before,
In sedulous recurrence to his trade
Whereby he earneth him the daily bread;
And studiously the humbler for that pride,
Professedly the faultier that he knows

God's secret, while he holds the thread of life.
Indeed the especial marking of the man
Is prone submission to the heavenly will—
Seeing it, what it is, and why it is.
'Sayeth, he will wait patient to the last
For that same death which must restore his being
To equilibrium, body loosening soul
Divorced even now by premature full growth:
He will live, nay, it pleaseth him to live
So long as God please, and just how God please.
He even seeketh not to please God more
(Which meaneth, otherwise) than as God please.
Hence, I perceive not he affects to preach
The doctrine of his sect whate'er it be,
Make proselytes as madmen thirst to do:
How can he give his neighbour the real ground,
His own conviction? Ardent as he is—
Call his great truth a lie, why, still the old
"Be it as God please" reassureth him.
I probed the sore as thy disciple should:
"How, beast," said I, "this stolid carelessness
Sufficeth thee, when Rome is on her march
To stamp out like a little spark thy town,
Thy tribe, thy crazy tale and thee at once?"
He merely looked with his large eyes on me.
The man is apathetic, you deduce?
Contrariwise, he loves both old and young,
Able and weak, affects the very brutes
And birds—how say I? flowers of the field—
As a wise workman recognizes tools
In a master's workshop, loving what they make.
Thus is the man as harmless as a lamb:
Only impatient, let him do his best,
At ignorance and carelessness and sin—
An indignation which is promptly curbed:
As when in certain travel I have feigned
To be an ignoramus in our art
According to some preconceived design,
And happed to hear the land's practitioners
Steeped in conceit sublimed by ignorance,

Prattle fantastically on disease,
Its cause and cure—and I must hold my peace!

   Thou wilt object—Why have I not ere this
Sought out the sage himself, the Nazarene
Who wrought this cure, inquiring at the source,
Conferring with the frankness that befits?
Alas! it grieveth me, the learned leech
Perished in a tumult many years ago,
Accused,—our learning's fate,—of wizardry,
Rebellion, to the setting up a rule
And creed prodigious as described to me.
His death, which happened when the earthquake fell
(Prefiguring, as soon appeared, the loss
To occult learning in our lord the sage
Who lived there in the pyramid alone)
Was wrought by the mad people—that's their wont!
On vain recourse, as I conjecture it,
To his tried virtue, for miraculous help—
How could he stop the earthquake? That's their way!
The other imputations must be lies:
But take one, tho' I loathe to give it thee,
In mere respect for any good man's fame.
(And after all, our patient Lazarus
Is stark mad; should we count on what he says?
Perhaps not: tho' in writing to a leech
'T is well to keep back nothing of a case.)
This man so cured regards the curer, then,
As—God forgive me! who but God himself,
Creator and sustainer of the world,
That came and dwelt in flesh on it awhile.
—'Sayeth that such an one was born and lived,
Taught, healed the sick, broke bread at his own house,
Then died, with Lazarus by, for aught I know,
And yet was . . . what I said nor choose repeat,
And must have so avouched himself, in fact,
In hearing of this very Lazarus
Who saith—but why all this of what he saith?
Why write of trivial matters, things of price
Calling at every moment for remark?

I noticed on the margin of a pool
Blue-flowering borage, the Aleppo sort,
Aboundeth, very nitrous. It is strange!

Thy pardon for this long and tedious case,
Which, now that I review it, needs must seem
Unduly dwelt on, prolixly set forth!
Nor I myself discern in what is writ
Good cause for the peculiar interest
And awe indeed this man has touched me with.
Perhaps the journey's end, the weariness
Had wrought upon me first. I met him thus:
I crossed a ridge of short sharp broken hills
Like an old lion's cheek teeth. Out there came
A moon made like a face with certain spots
Multiform, manifold and menacing:
Then a wind rose behind me. So we met
In this old sleepy town at unaware,
The man and I. I send thee what is writ.
Regard it as a chance, a matter risked
To this ambiguous Syrian: he may lose,
Or steal, or give it thee with equal good.
Jerusalem's repose shall make amends
For time this letter wastes, thy time and mine;
Till when, once more thy pardon and farewell!

The very God! think, Abib; dost thou think?
So, the All-Great, were the All-Loving too—
So, thro' the thunder comes a human voice
Saying, "O heart I made, a heart beats here!
Face, my hands fashioned, see it in myself!
Thou hast no power nor mayst conceive of mine:
But love I gave thee, with myself to love,
And thou must love me who have died for thee!"
The madman saith He said so: it is strange.

A Serenade at the Villa

1   That was I, you heard last night,
        When there rose no moon at all,

Nor, to pierce the strained and tight
   Tent of heaven, a planet small:
Life was dead, and so was light.

II   Not a twinkle from the fly,
     Not a glimmer from the worm;
When the crickets stopped their cry,
     When the owls forbore a term,
You heard music; that was I.

III   Earth turned in her sleep with pain,
     Sultrily suspired for proof:
In at heaven and out again,
     Lightning!—where it broke the roof,
Bloodlike, some few drops of rain.

IV   What they could my words expressed,
     O my love, my all, my one!
Singing helped the verses best,
     And when singing's best was done,
To my lute I left the rest.

V   So wore night; the East was gray,
     White the broad-faced hemlock flowers:
There would be another day;
     Ere its first of heavy hours
Found me, I had passed away.

VI   What became of all the hopes,
     Words and song and lute as well?
Say, this struck you: "When life gropes
     Feebly for the path where fell
Light last on the evening slopes,—

VII   "One friend in that path shall be,
     To secure my step from wrong;
One to count night day for me,
     Patient through the watches long,
Serving most with none to see."

VIII   Never say—as something bodes—
     "So, the worst has yet a worse!

When life halts 'neath double loads,
    Better the task-master's curse
Than such music on the roads!

IX   "When no moon succeeds the sun,
        Nor can pierce the midnight's tent
    Any star, the smallest one,
        While some drops, where lightning rent,
    Show the final storm begun—

X   "When the fire-fly hides its spot,
        When the garden-voices fail
    In the darkness thick and hot,—
        Shall another voice avail,
    That shape be where these are not?

XI   "Has some plague a longer lease,
        Proffering its help uncouth?
    Can't one even die in peace?
        As one shuts one's eyes on youth,
    Is that face the last one sees?"

XII Oh how dark your villa was,
        Windows fast and obdurate!
    How the garden grudged me grass
        Where I stood—the iron gate
    Ground its teeth to let me pass!

My Star

All that I know
    Of a certain star
Is, it can throw
    (Like the angled spar)
Now a dart of red,
    Now a dart of blue;
Till my friends have said
    They would fain see, too,

My star that dartles the red and the blue!
Then it stops like a bird; like a flower, hangs furled:
   They must solace themselves with the Saturn above it.
What matter to me if their star is a world?
   Mine has opened its soul to me; therefore I love it.

"Childe Roland to the Dark Tower Came"

(SEE EDGAR'S SONG IN *LEAR*)

I   My first thought was, he lied in every word,
      That hoary cripple, with malicious eye
      Askance to watch the working of his lie
On mine, and mouth scarce able to afford
Suppression of the glee, that pursed and scored
      Its edge, at one more victim gained thereby.

II   What else should he be set for, with his staff?
      What, save to waylay with his lies, ensnare
      All travelers who might find him posted there,
And ask the road? I guessed what skull-like laugh
Would break, what crutch 'gin write my epitaph
      For pastime in the dusty thoroughfare,

III   If at his counsel I should turn aside
      Into that ominous tract which, all agree,
      Hides the Dark Tower. Yet acquiescingly
I did turn as he pointed: neither pride
Nor hope rekindling at the end descried,
      So much as gladness that some end might be.

IV   For, what with my whole world-wide wandering,
      What with my search drawn out thro' years, my hope
      Dwindled into a ghost not fit to cope
With that obstreperous joy success would bring,—
I hardly tried now to rebuke the spring
      My heart made, finding failure in its scope.

v   As when a sick man very near to death
       Seems dead indeed, and feels begin and end
       The tears and takes the farewell of each friend,
     And hears one bid the other go, draw breath
     Freelier outside, ("since all is o'er," he saith,
       "And the blow fallen no grieving can amend;")

vi   While some discuss if near the other graves
       Be room enough for this, and when a day
       Suits best for carrying the corpse away,
     With care about the banners, scarves and staves:
     And still the man hears all, and only craves
       He may not shame such tender love and stay.

vii Thus, I had so long suffered in this quest,
       Heard failure prophesied so oft, been writ
       So many times among "The Band"—to wit,
     The knights who to the Dark Tower's search addressed
     Their steps—that just to fail as they, seemed best,
       And all the doubt was now—should I be fit?

viii So, quiet as despair, I turned from him,
       That hateful cripple, out of his highway
       Into the path he pointed. All the day
     Had been a dreary one at best, and dim
     Was settling to its close, yet shot one grim
       Red leer to see the plain catch its estray. [1]

ix   For mark! no sooner was I fairly found
       Pledged to the plain, after a pace or two,
       Than, pausing to throw backward a last view
     O'er the safe road, 't was gone; gray plain all round:
     Nothing but plain to the horizon's bound.
       I might go on; naught else remained to do.

x   So, on I went. I think I never saw
       Such starved ignoble nature; nothing throve:
       For flowers—as well expect a cedar grove!

---

[1] Stray animal.

But cockle, spurge, according to their law
Might propagate their kind, with none to awe,
   You'd think; a burr had been a treasure trove.

XI No! penury, inertness and grimace,
     In some strange sort, were the land's portion. "See
     Or shut your eyes," said Nature peevishly,
    "It nothing skills: I can not help my case:
    'T is the Last Judgment's fire must cure this place,
     Calcine its clods and set my prisoners free."

XII If there pushed any ragged thistle-stalk
     Above its mates, the head was chopped; the bents[1]
     Were jealous else. What made those holes and rents
    In the dock's harsh swarth leaves, bruised as to balk
    All hope of greenness? 't is a brute must walk
     Pashing their life out, with a brute's intents.

XIII As for the grass, it grew as scant as hair
     In leprosy; thin dry blades pricked the mud
     Which underneath looked kneaded up with blood.
    One stiff blind horse, his every bone a-stare,
    Stood stupefied, however he came there:
     Thrust out past service from the devil's stud!

XIV Alive? he might be dead for aught I know,
     With that red gaunt and colloped[2] neck a-strain,
     And shut eyes underneath the rusty mane;
    Seldom went such grotesqueness with such woe;
    I never saw a brute I hated so;
     He must be wicked to deserve such pain.

XV I shut my eyes and turned them on my heart.
     As a man calls for wine before he fights,
     I asked one draught of earlier, happier sights,
    Ere fitly I could hope to play my part.
    Think first, fight afterwards—the soldier's art:
     One taste of the old time sets all to rights.

[1] Coarse grasses.
[2] (?) With skin lying in folds.

XVI Not it! I fancied Cuthbert's reddening face
   Beneath its garniture of curly gold,
   Dear fellow, till I almost felt him fold
 An arm in mine to fix me to the place,
 That way he used. Alas, one night's disgrace!
   Out went my heart's new fire and left it cold.

XVII Giles then, the soul of honour—there he stands
   Frank as ten years ago when knighted first.
   What honest man should dare (he said) he durst.
 Good—but the scene shifts—faugh! what hangman hands
 Pin to his breast a parchment? His own bands
   Read it. Poor traitor, spit upon and curst!

XVIII Better this present than a past like that;
   Back therefore to my darkening path again!
   No sound, no sight as far as eye could strain.
 Will the night send a howlet[1] or a bat?
 I asked: when something on the dismal flat
   Came to arrest my thoughts and change their train.

XIX A sudden little river crossed my path
   As unexpected as a serpent comes.
   No sluggish tide congenial to the glooms;
 This, as it frothed by, might have been a bath
 For the fiend's glowing hoof—to see the wrath
   Of its black eddy bespate with flakes and spumes.

XX So petty yet so spiteful! All along,
   Low scrubby alders kneeled down over it;
   Drenched willows flung them headlong in a fit
 Of mute despair, a suicidal throng:
 The river which had done them all the wrong,
   Whate'er that was, rolled by, deterred no whit.

XXI Which, while I forded,—good saints, how I feared
   To set my foot upon a dead man's cheek,
   Each step, or feel the spear I thrust to seek

---

[1] Owl.

For hollows, tangled in his hair or beard!
—It may have been a water-rat I speared,
But, ugh! it sounded like a baby's shriek.

XXII   Glad was I when I reached the other bank.
Now for a better country. Vain presage!
Who were the strugglers, what war did they wage
Whose savage trample thus could pad the dank
Soil to a plash? Toads in a poisoned tank,
Or wild cats in a red-hot iron cage—

XXIII   The fight must so have seemed in that fell cirque.[1]
What penned them there, with all the plain to choose?
No foot-print leading to that horrid mews,
None out of it. Mad brewage set to work
Their brains, no doubt, like galley-slaves the Turk
Pits for his pastime, Christians against Jews.

XXIV   And more than that—a furlong on—why, there!
What bad use was that engine for, that wheel,
Or brake,[2] not wheel—that harrow fit to reel
Men's bodies out like silk? with all the air
Of Tophet's[3] tool, on earth left unaware,
Or brought to sharpen its rusty teeth of steel.

XXV   Then came a bit of stubbed ground, once a wood,
Next a marsh, it would seem, and now mere earth
Desperate and done with; (so a fool finds mirth,
Makes a thing and then mars it, till his mood
Changes and off he goes!) within a rood[4]—
Bog, clay, and rubble, sand and stark black dearth.

XXVI   Now blotches rankling, coloured gay and grim,
Now patches where some leanness of the soil's
Broke into moss or substances like boils;
Then came some palsied oak, a cleft in him
Like a distorted mouth that splits its rim
Gaping at death, and dies while it recoils.

---

[1] Circus, amphitheater.
[2] Harrow.
[3] Hell's.
[4] Quarter of an acre.

XXVII   And just as far as ever from the end,
      Naught in the distance but the evening, naught
      To point my footstep further! At the thought,
  A great black bird, Apollyon's[1] bosom-friend,
  Sailed past, nor beat his wide wing dragon-penned
      That brushed my cap—perchance the guide I sought.

XXVIII   For, looking up, aware I somehow grew,
      'Spite of the dusk, the plain had given place
      All round to mountains—with such name to grace
  Mere ugly heights and heaps now stolen in view.
  How thus they had surprised me,—solve it, you!
      How to get from them was no clearer case.

XXIX   Yet half I seemed to recognize some trick
      Of mischief happened to me, God knows when—
      In a bad dream perhaps. Here ended, then,
  Progress this way. When, in the very nick
  Of giving up, one time more, came a click
      As when a trap shuts—you're inside the den.

XXX   Burningly it came on me all at once,
      This was the place! those two hills on the right,
      Crouched like two bulls locked horn in horn in fight,
  While, to the left, a tall scalped mountain . . . Dunce,
  Dotard, a-dozing at the very nonce,
      After a life spent training for the sight!

XXXI   What in the midst lay but the Tower itself?
      The round squat turret, blind as the fool's heart,
      Built of brown stone, without a counterpart
  In the whole world. The tempest's mocking elf
  Points to the shipman thus the unseen shelf
      He strikes on, only when the timbers start.

XXXII   Not see? because of night perhaps?—why, day
      Came back again for that! before it left,
      The dying sunset kindled thro' a cleft:

---

[1] The devil's.

The hills, like giants at a hunting, lay,
Chin upon hand, to see the game at bay,—
    "Now stab and end the creature—to the heft!"

XXXIII Not hear? when noise was everywhere! it tolled
            Increasing like a bell. Names in my ears
            Of all the lost adventurers my peers,—
        How such a one was strong, and such was bold,
        And such was fortunate, yet each of old
            Lost, lost! one moment knelled the woe of years.

XXXIV There they stood, ranged along the hill-sides, met
            To view the last of me, a living frame
            For one more picture! in a sheet of flame
        I saw them and I knew them all. And yet
        Dauntless the slug-horn to my lips I set,
            And blew *"Childe Roland to the Dark Tower came."*

Love in a Life

I   Room after room,
    I hunt the house through
    We inhabit together.
    Heart, fear nothing, for, heart, thou shalt find her—
    Next time, herself!—not the trouble behind her
    Left in the curtain, the couch's perfume!
    As she brushed it, the cornice-wreath blossomed anew;
    Yon looking-glass gleamed at the wave of her feather.

II Yet the day wears,
    And door succeeds door;
    I try the fresh fortune—
    Range the wide house from the wing to the centre.
    Still the same chance! she goes out as I enter.
    Spend my whole day in the quest,—who cares?
    But 't is twilight, you see,—with such suites to explore,
    Such closets to search, such alcoves to importune!

How It Strikes a Contemporary

I only knew one poet in my life:
And this, or something like it, was his way.

    You saw go up and down Valladolid,
A man of mark, to know next time you saw.
His very serviceable suit of black
Was courtly once and conscientious still,
And many might have worn it, tho' none did:
The cloak, that somewhat shone and showed the threads,
Had purpose, and the ruff, significance.
He walked, and tapped the pavement with his cane,
Scenting the world, looking it full in face,
An old dog, bald and blindish, at his heels.
They turned up, now, the alley by the church,
That leads no whither; now, they breathed themselves
On the main promenade just at the wrong time:
You'd come upon his scrutinizing hat,
Making a peaked shade blacker than itself
Against the single window spared some house
Intact yet with its mouldered Moorish work, —
Or else surprise the ferrel of his stick
Trying the mortar's temper 'tween the chinks
Of some new shop a-building, French and fine.
He stood and watched the cobbler at his trade,
The man who slices lemons into drink,
The coffee-roaster's brazier, and the boys
That volunteer to help him turn its winch.
He glanced o'er books on stalls with half an eye,
And fly-leaf ballads on the vendor's string,
And broad-edge bold-print posters by the wall.
He took such cognizance of men and things,
If any beat a horse, you felt he saw;
If any cursed a woman, he took note;
Yet stared at nobody, —you stared at him,
And found, less to your pleasure than surprise,
He seemed to know you and expect as much.
So, next time that a neighbour's tongue was loosed,

It marked the shameful and notorious fact
We had among us, not so much a spy
As a recording chief-inquisitor,
The town's true master if the town but knew!
We merely kept a governor for form,
While this man walked about and took account
Of all thought, said and acted, then went home,
And wrote it fully to our Lord the King
Who has an itch to know things, he knows why,
And reads them in his bed-room of a night.
Oh, you might smile! there wanted not a touch,
A tang of . . . well, it was not wholly ease
As back into your mind the man's look came.
Stricken in years a little—such a brow
His eyes had to live under!—clear as flint
On either side the formidable nose
Curved, cut and coloured like an eagle's claw.
Had he to do with A's surprising fate?
When altogether old B disappeared
And young C got his mistress,—was't our friend,
His letter to the King, that did it all?
What paid the bloodless man for so much pains?
Our Lord the King has favourites manifold,
And shifts his ministry some once a month;
Our city gets new governors at whiles,—
But never word or sign, that I could hear,
Notified to this man about the streets,
The King's approval of those letters conned
The last thing duly at the dead of night.
Did the man love his office? Frowned our Lord,
Exhorting when none heard—"Beseech me not!
Too far above my people,—beneath me!
I set the watch,—how should the people know?
Forget them, keep me all the more in mind!"
Was some such understanding 'twixt the two?

I found no truth in one report at least—
That if you tracked him to his home, down lanes
Beyond the Jewry, and as clean to pace,
You found he ate his supper in a room
Blazing with lights, four Titians on the wall,

And twenty naked girls to change his plate!
Poor man, he lived another kind of life
In that new stuccoed third house by the bridge,
Fresh-painted, rather smart than otherwise!
The whole street might o'erlook him as he sat,
Leg crossing leg, one foot on the dog's back,
Playing a decent cribbage with his maid
(Jacynth, you're sure her name was) o'er the cheese
And fruit, three red halves of starved winter-pears,
Or treat of radishes in April. Nine,
Ten, struck the church clock, straight to bed went he.

    My father, like the man of sense he was,
Would point him out to me a dozen times;
"St—St," he'd whisper, "the Corregidor!"[1]
I had been used to think that personage
Was one with lacquered breeches, lustrous belt,
And feathers like a forest in his hat,
Who blew a trumpet and proclaimed the news,
Announced the bull-fights, gave each church its turn,
And memorized[2] the miracle in vogue!
He had a great observance from us boys;
We were in error; that was not the man.

    I'd like now, yet had haply been afraid,
To have just looked, when this man came to die,
And seen who lined the clean gay garret sides,
And stood about the neat low truckle-bed,
With the heavenly manner of relieving guard.
Here had been, mark, the general-in-chief,
Thro' a whole campaign of the world's life and death,
Doing the King's work all the dim day long,
In his old coat and up to knees in mud,
Smoked like a herring, dining on a crust,—
And, now the day was won, relieved at once!
No further show or need for that old coat,
You are sure, for one thing! Bless us, all the while
How sprucely we are dressed out, you and I!
A second, and the angels alter that.

---

[1] Chief magistrate.
[2] Memorialized.

Well, I could never write a verse,—could you?
Let's to the Prado¹ and make the most of time.

The Last Ride Together

I   I said—Then, dearest, since 't is so,
    Since now at length my fate I know,
    Since nothing all my love avails,
    Since all, my life seemed meant for, fails,
      Since this was written and needs must be—
    My whole heart rises up to bless
    Your name in pride and thankfulness!
    Take back the hope you gave,—I claim
    Only a memory of the same,
    —And this beside, if you will not blame,
      Your leave for one more last ride with me.

II   My mistress bent that brow of hers;
    Those deep dark eyes where pride demurs
    When pity would be softening through,
    Fixed me a breathing-while or two
      With life or death in the balance: right!
    The blood replenished me again;
    My last thought was at least not vain:
    I and my mistress, side by side
    Shall be together, breathe and ride,
    So, one day more am I deified.
      Who knows but the world may end to-night?

III   Hush! if you saw some western cloud
    All billowy-bosomed, over-bowed
    By many benedictions—sun's
    And moon's and evening star's at once—
      And so, you, looking and loving best,
    Conscious grew, your passion drew
    Cloud, sunset, moonrise, star-shine too,

¹ A fashionable promenade.

Down on you, near and yet more near,
Till flesh must fade for heaven was here!—
Thus leant she and lingered—joy and fear!
    Thus lay she a moment on my breast.

IV   Then we began to ride. My soul
Smoothed itself out, a long-cramped scroll
Freshening and fluttering in the wind.
Past hopes already lay behind.
    What need to strive with a life awry?
Had I said that, had I done this,
So might I gain, so might I miss.
Might she have loved me? just as well
She might have hated, who can tell!
Where had I been now if the worst befell?
    And here we are riding, she and I.

V   Fail I alone, in words and deeds?
Why, all men strive and who succeeds?
We rode; it seemed my spirit flew,
Saw other regions, cities new,
    As the world rushed by on either side.
I thought,—All labour, yet no less
Bear up beneath their unsuccess.
Look at the end of work, contrast
The petty done, the undone vast,
This present of theirs with the hopeful past!
    I hoped she would love me; here we ride.

VI   What hand and brain went ever paired?
What heart alike conceived and dared?
What act proved all its thought had been?
What will but felt the fleshly screen?
    We ride and I see her bosom heave.
There's many a crown for who can reach.
Ten lines, a statesman's life in each!
The flag stuck on a heap of bones,
A soldier's doing! what atones?
They scratch his name on the Abbey-stones.
    My riding is better, by their leave.

VII   What does it all mean, poet? Well,
Your brains beat into rhythm, you tell
What we felt only; you expressed
You hold things beautiful the best,
    And pace them in rhyme so, side by side.
'T is something, nay 't is much: but then,
Have you yourself what's best for men?
Are you—poor, sick, old ere your time—
Nearer one whit your own sublime
Than we who never have turned a rhyme?
    Sing, riding's a joy! For me, I ride.

VIII   And you, great sculptor—so, you gave
A score of years to Art, her slave,
And that's your Venus, whence we turn
To yonder girl that fords the burn!
    You acquiesce, and shall I repine?
What, man of music, you grown gray
With notes and nothing else to say,
Is this your sole praise from a friend,
"Greatly his opera's strains intend,
But in music we know how fashions end!"
    I gave my youth; but we ride, in fine.

IX   Who knows what's fit for us? Had fate
Proposed bliss here should sublimate
My being—had I signed the bond—
Still one must lead some life beyond,
    Have a bliss to die with, dim-descried.
This foot once planted on the goal,
This glory-garland round my soul,
Could I descry such? Try and test!
I sink back shuddering from the quest.
Earth being so good, would heaven seem best?
    Now, heaven and she are beyond this ride.

X   And yet—she has not spoke so long!
What if heaven be that, fair and strong
At life's best, with our eyes upturned
Whither life's flower is first discerned,
    We, fixed so, ever should so abide?

What if we still ride on, we two,
With life for ever old yet new,
Changed not in kind but in degree,
The instant made eternity,—
And heaven just prove that I and she
    Ride, ride together, for ever ride?

The Patriot

AN OLD STORY

I   It was roses, roses, all the way,
      With myrtle mixed in my path like mad:
  The house-roofs seemed to heave and sway,
      The church-spires flamed, such flags they had,
  A year ago on this very day.

II   The air broke into a mist with bells,
      The old walls rocked with the crowd and cries.
  Had I said, "Good folk, mere noise repels—
      But give me your sun from yonder skies!"
  They had answered "And afterward, what else?"

III   Alack, it was I who leaped at the sun
      To give it my loving friends to keep!
  Naught man could do, have I left undone:
      And you see my harvest, what I reap
  This very day, now a year is run.

IV   There's nobody on the house-tops now—
      Just a palsied few at the windows set;
  For the best of the sight is, all allow,
      At the Shambles' Gate—or, better yet,
  By the very scaffold's foot, I trow.

V   I go in the rain, and, more than needs,
      A rope cuts both my wrists behind;
  And I think, by the feel, my forehead bleeds,
      For they fling, whoever has a mind,
  Stones at me for my year's misdeeds.

VI Thus I entered, and thus I go!
  In triumphs, people have dropped down dead.
  "Paid by the world, what dost thou owe
    Me?"—God might question; now instead,
  'T is God shall repay: I am safer so.

Memorabilia

I Ah, did you once see Shelley plain,
    And did he stop and speak to you
  And did you speak to him again?
    How strange it seems and new!

II But you were living before that,
    And also you are living after;
  And the memory I started at—
    My starting moves your laughter!

III I crossed a moor, with a name of its own
    And a certain use in the world, no doubt,
  Yet a hand's-breadth of it shines alone
    'Mid the blank miles round about:

IV For there I picked up on the heather
    And there I put inside my breast
  A moulted feather, an eagle-feather!
    Well, I forget the rest.

Andrea del Sarto[1]

(CALLED "THE FAULTLESS PAINTER")

But do not let us quarrel any more,
No, my Lucrezia! bear with me for once:
Sit down and all shall happen as you wish.
You turn your face, but does it bring your heart?

---

[1] The sixteenth-century Florentine painter, called "del Sarto" because he was the son of a tailor.

I'll work then for your friend's friend, never fear,
Treat his own subject after his own way,
Fix his own time, accept too his own price,
And shut the money into this small hand
When next it takes mine. Will it? tenderly?
Oh, I'll content him,—but to-morrow, Love!
I often am much wearier than you think,
This evening more than usual: and it seems
As if—forgive now—should you let me sit
Here by the window, with your hand in mine,
And look a half-hour forth on Fiesole,
Both of one mind, as married people use,
Quietly, quietly the evening through,
I might get up to-morrow to my work
Cheerful and fresh as ever. Let us try.
To-morrow, how you shall be glad for this!
Your soft hand is a woman of itself,
And mine the man's bared breast she curls inside.
Don't count the time lost, neither; you must serve
For each of the five pictures we require:
It saves a model. So! keep looking so—
My serpentining beauty, rounds on rounds!
—How could you ever prick those perfect ears,
Even to put the pearl there! oh, so sweet—
My face, my moon, my everybody's moon,
Which everybody looks on and calls his,
And, I suppose, is looked on by in turn,
While she looks—no one's: very dear, no less.
You smile? why, there's my picture ready made,
There's what we painters call our harmony!
A common grayness silvers everything,—
All in a twilight, you and I alike
—You, at the point of your first pride in me
(That's gone, you know)—but I, at every point;
My youth, my hope, my art, being all toned down
To yonder sober pleasant Fiesole.
There's the bell clinking from the chapel-top;
That length of convent-wall across the way
Holds the trees safer, huddled more inside;
The last monk leaves the garden; days decrease,
And autumn grows, autumn in everything.

Eh? the whole seems to fall into a shape,
As if I saw alike my work and self
And all that I was born to be and do,
A twilight-piece. Love, we are in God's hand.
How strange now, looks the life he makes us lead;
So free we seem, so fettered fast we are!
I feel he laid the fetter: let it lie!
This chamber for example—turn your head—
All that's behind us! You don't understand
Nor care to understand about my art,
But you can hear at least when people speak:
And that cartoon, the second from the door
—It is the thing, Love! so such things should be— .
Behold Madonna!—I am bold to say.
I can do with my pencil what I know,
What I see, what at bottom of my heart
I wish for, if I ever wish so deep—
Do easily, too—when I say, perfectly,
I do not boast, perhaps: yourself are judge,
Who listened to the Legate's talk last week;
And just as much they used to say in France.
At any rate 't is easy, all of it!
No sketches first, no studies, that's long past:
I do what many dream of, all their lives,
—Dream? strive to do, and agonize to do,
And fail in doing. I could count twenty such
On twice your fingers, and not leave this town,
Who strive—you don't know how the others strive
To paint a little thing like that you smeared
Carelessly passing with your robes afloat,—
Yet do much less, so much less, Someone says,
(I know his name, no matter)—so much less!
Well, less is more, Lucrezia: I am judged.
There burns a truer light of God in them,
In their vexed beating stuffed and stopped-up brain,
Heart, or whate'er else, than goes on to prompt
This low-pulsed forthright craftsman's hand of mine.
Their works drop groundward, but themselves, I know,
Reach many a time a heaven that's shut to me,
Enter and take their place there sure enough,
Tho' they come back and cannot tell the world.

My works are nearer heaven, but I sit here.
The sudden blood of these men! at a word—
Praise them, it boils, or blame them, it boils too.
I, painting from myself and to myself,
Know what I do, am unmoved by men's blame
Or their praise either. Somebody remarks
Morello's outline there is wrongly traced,
His hue mistaken; what of that? or else,
Rightly traced and well ordered; what of that?
Speak as they please, what does the mountain care?
Ah, but a man's reach should exceed his grasp,
Or what's a heaven for? All is silver-gray,
Placid and perfect with my art: the worse!
I know both what I want and what might gain,
And yet how profitless to know, to sigh
"Had I been two, another and myself,
Our head would have o'erlooked the world!" No doubt.
Yonder's a work now, of that famous youth
The Urbinate[1] who died five years ago.
('T is copied, George Vasari sent it me.)
Well, I can fancy how he did it all,
Pouring his soul, with kings and popes to see,
Reaching, that heaven might so replenish him,
Above and thro' his art—for it gives way;
That arm is wrongly put—and there again—
A fault to pardon in the drawing's lines,
Its body, so to speak: its soul is right,
He means right—that, a child may understand.
Still, what an arm! and I could alter it:
But all the play, the insight and the stretch—
Out of me, out of me! And wherefore out?
Had you enjoined them on me, given me soul,
We might have risen to Rafael, I and you!
Nay, Love, you did give all I asked, I think—
More than I merit, yes, by many times.
But had you—oh, with the same perfect brow,
And perfect eyes, and more than perfect mouth,
And the low voice my soul hears, as a bird
The fowler's pipe, and follows to the snare—

---

[1] Raphael, who was born in Urbino.

Had you, with these the same, but brought a mind!
Some women do so. Had the mouth there urged
"God and the glory! never care for gain.
The present by the future, what is that?
Live for fame, side by side with Agnolo![1]
Rafael is waiting: up to God, all three!"
I might have done it for you. So it seems:
Perhaps not. All is as God over-rules.
Beside, incentives come from the soul's self;
The rest avail not. Why do I need you?
What wife had Rafael, or has Agnolo?
In this world, who can do a thing, will not;
And who would do it, can not, I perceive:
Yet the will's somewhat—somewhat, too, the power
And thus we half-men struggle. At the end,
God, I conclude, compensates, punishes.
'T is safer for me, if the award be strict,
That I am something underrated here,
Poor this long while, despised, to speak the truth.
I dared not, do you know, leave home all day,
For fear of chancing on the Paris lords.
The best is when they pass and look aside;
But they speak sometimes; I must bear it all.
Well may they speak! That Francis, that first time,
And that long festal year at Fontainebleau!
I surely then could sometimes leave the ground,
Put on the glory, Rafael's daily wear,
In that humane great monarch's golden look,—
One finger in his beard or twisted curl
Over his mouth's good mark that made the smile,
One arm about my shoulder, round my neck,
The jingle of his gold chain in my ear,
I painting proudly with his breath on me,
All his court round him, seeing with his eyes,
Such frank French eyes, and such a fire of souls
Profuse, my hand kept plying by those hearts,—
And, best of all, this, this, this face beyond,
This in the background, waiting on my work,
To crown the issue with a last reward!

---

[1] Michelangelo.

A good time, was it not, my kingly days?
And had you not grown restless . . . but I know—
'T is done and past; 't was right, my instinct said;
Too live the life grew, golden and not gray:
And I'm the weak-eyed bat no sun should tempt
Out of the grange whose four walls make his world.
How could it end in any other way?
You called me, and I came home to your heart.
The triumph was—to reach and stay there; since
I reached it ere the triumph, what is lost?
Let my hands frame your face in your hair's gold,
You beautiful Lucrezia that are mine!
"Rafael did this, Andrea painted that;
The Roman's is the better when you pray,
But still the other's Virgin was his wife—"
Men will excuse me. I am glad to judge
Both pictures in your presence; clearer grows
My better fortune, I resolve to think.
For, do you know, Lucrezia, as God lives,
Said one day Agnolo, his very self,
To Rafael . . . I have known it all these years . . .
(When the young man was flaming out his thoughts
Upon a palace-wall for Rome to see,
Too lifted up in heart because of it)
"Friend, there's a certain sorry little scrub
Goes up and down our Florence, none cares how,
Who, were he set to plan and execute
As you are, pricked on by your popes and kings,
Would bring the sweat into that brow of yours!"
To Rafael's!—And indeed the arm is wrong.
I hardly dare . . . yet, only you to see,
Give the chalk here—quick, thus the line should go!
Ay, but the soul! he's Rafael! rub it out!
Still, all I care for, if he spoke the truth,
(What he? why, who but Michel Agnolo?
Do you forget already words like those?)
If really there was such a chance so lost,—
Is, whether you're—not grateful—but more pleased.
Well, let me think so. And you smile indeed!
This hour has been an hour! Another smile?
If you would sit thus by me every night

I should work better, do you comprehend?
I mean that I should earn more, give you more.
See, it is settled dusk now; there's a star;
Morello's gone, the watch-lights show the wall,
The cue-owls[1] speak the name we call them by.
Come from the window, love,—come in, at last,
Inside the melancholy little house
We built to be so gay with. God is just.
King Francis may forgive me: oft at nights
When I look up from painting, eyes tired out,
The walls become illumined, brick from brick
Distinct, instead of mortar, fierce bright gold,
That gold of his I did cement them with!
Let us but love each other. Must you go?
That Cousin here again? he waits outside?
Must see you—you, and not with me? Those loans?
More gaming debts to pay? you smiled for that?
Well, let smiles buy me! have you more to spend?
While hand and eye and something of a heart
Are left me, work's my ware, and what's it worth?
I'll pay my fancy. Only let me sit
The gray remainder of the evening out,
Idle, you call it, and muse perfectly
How I could paint, were I but back in France,
One picture, just one more—the Virgin's face,
Not yours this time! I want you at my side
To hear them—that is, Michel Agnolo—
Judge all I do and tell you of its worth.
Will you? To-morrow, satisfy your friend.
I take the subjects for his corridor,
Finish the portrait out of hand—there, there,
And throw him in another thing or two
If he demurs; the whole should prove enough
To pay for this same Cousin's freak. Beside,
What's better and what's all I care about,
Get you the thirteen scudi for the ruff!
Love, does that please you? Ah, but what does he,
The Cousin! what does he to please you more?

---

[1] Scops owls.

I am grown peaceful as old age to-night.
I regret little, I would change still less.
Since there my past life lies, why alter it?
The very wrong to Francis!—it is true
I took his coin, was tempted and complied,
And built this house and sinned, and all is said.
My father and my mother died of want.
Well, had I riches of my own? you see
How one gets rich! Let each one bear his lot.
They were born poor, lived poor, and poor they died:
And I have laboured somewhat in my time
And not been paid profusely. Some good son
Paint my two hundred pictures—let him try!
No doubt, there's something strikes a balance. Yes,
You loved me quite enough, it seems to-night.
This must suffice me here. What would one have?
In heaven, perhaps, new chances, one more chance—
Four great walls in the New Jerusalem,
Meted on each side by the angel's reed,
For Leonard,[1] Rafael, Agnolo and me
To cover—the three first without a wife,
While I have mine! So—still they overcome
Because there's still Lucrezia,—as I choose.

Again the Cousin's whistle! Go, my Love.

In a Year

I   Never any more,
        While I live,
     Need I hope to see his face
        As before.
     Once his love grown chill,
        Mine may strive:
     Bitterly we re-embrace,
        Single still.

II Was it something said,
        Something done,

---

[1] Leonardo da Vinci.

Vexed him? was it touch of hand,
  Turn of head?
Strange! that very way
  Love begun:
I as little understand
  Love's decay.

III When I sewed or drew,
    I recall
How he looked as if I sung,
    —Sweetly too.
If I spoke a word,
    First of all
Up his cheek the colour sprung,
    Then he heard.

IV Sitting by my side,
    At my feet,
So he breathed but air I breathed,
    Satisfied!
I, too, at love's brim
    Touched the sweet:
I would die if death bequeathed
    Sweet to him.

V "Speak, I love thee best!"
    He exclaimed:
"Let thy love my own foretell!"
    I confessed:
"Clasp my heart on thine
    Now unblamed,
Since upon thy soul as well
    Hangeth mine!"

VI Was it wrong to own,
    Being truth?
Why should all the giving prove
    His alone?
I had wealth and ease,
    Beauty, youth:
Since my lover gave me love,
    I gave these.

VII   That was all I meant,
      —To be just,
  And the passion I had raised,
      To content.
  Since he chose to change
      Gold for dust,
  If I gave him what he praised
      Was it strange?

VIII   Would he loved me yet,
      On and on,
  While I found some way undreamed
      —Paid my debt!
  Gave more life and more,
      Till all gone,
  He should smile "She never seemed
      Mine before.

IX   "What, she felt the while,
      Must I think?
  Love's so different with us men!"
      He should smile:
  "Dying for my sake—
      White and pink!
  Can't we touch these bubbles then
      But they break?"

X   Dear, the pang is brief,
      Do thy part,
  Have thy pleasure! How perplexed
      Grows belief!
  Well, this cold clay clod
      Was man's heart:
  Crumble it, and what comes next?
      Is it God?

Two in the Campagna

I   I wonder do you feel to-day
      As I have felt since, hand in hand,

We sat down on the grass, to stray
   In spirit better thro' the land,
This morn of Rome and May?

II   For me, I touched a thought, I know,
     Has tantalized me many times,
   (Like turns of thread the spiders throw
     Mocking across our path) for rhymes
To catch at and let go.

III   Help me to hold it! First it left
     The yellowing fennel, run to seed
There, branching from the brickwork's cleft,
     Some old tomb's ruin: yonder weed
Took up the floating weft,

IV   Where one small orange cup amassed
     Five beetles,—blind and green they grope
Among the honey-meal: and last,
     Everywhere on the grassy slope,
I traced it. Hold it fast!

V   The champaign with its endless fleece
     Of feathery grasses everywhere!
Silence and passion, joy and peace,
     An everlasting wash of air—
Rome's ghost since her decease.

VI   Such life here, thro' such lengths of hours,
     Such miracles performed in play,
Such primal naked forms of flowers,
     Such letting nature have her way
While heaven looks from its towers!

VII   How say you? Let us, O my dove,
     Let us be unashamed of soul,
As earth lies bare to heaven above!
     How is it under our control
To love or not to love?

VIII   I would that you were all to me,
     You that are just so much, no more.

Nor yours nor mine, nor slave nor free!
    Where does the fault lie? What the core
O' the wound, since wound must be?

IX   I would I could adopt your will,
    See with your eyes, and set my heart
Beating by yours, and drink my fill
    At your soul's springs,—your part my part
In life, for good and ill.

X   No. I yearn upward, touch you close,
    Then stand away. I kiss your cheek,
Catch your soul's warmth,—I pluck the rose
    And love it more than tongue can speak—
Then the good minute goes.

XI   Already how am I so far
    Out of that minute? Must I go
Still like the thistle-ball, no bar,
    Onward, whenever light winds blow,
Fixed by no friendly star?

XII   Just when I seemed about to learn!
    Where is the thread now? Off again.
The old trick! Only I discern—
    Infinite passion, and the pain
Of finite hearts that yearn.

A Grammarian's Funeral

SHORTLY AFTER THE REVIVAL OF LEARNING IN EUROPE

Let us begin and carry up this corpse,
    Singing together.
Leave we the common crofts, the vulgar thorpes,
    Each in its tether
Sleeping safe on the bosom of the plain,
    Cared-for till cock-crow:
Look out if yonder be not day again
    Rimming the rock-row!

That's the appropriate country; there, man's thought,
    Rarer, intenser,
Self-gathered for an outbreak, as it ought,
    Chafes in the censer.
Leave we the unlettered plain its herd and crop;
    Seek we sepulture
On a tall mountain, citied to the top,
    Crowded with culture!
All the peaks soar, but one the rest excels;
    Clouds overcome it;
No! yonder sparkle is the citadel's
    Circling its summit.
Thither our path lies; wind we up the heights:
    Wait ye the warning?
Our low life was the level's and the night's:
    He's for the morning.
Step to a tune, square chests, erect each head,
    'Ware the beholders!
This is our master, famous calm and dead,
    Borne on our shoulders.

Sleep, crop and herd! sleep, darkling thorpe and croft
    Safe from the weather!
He, whom we convoy to his grave aloft,
    Singing together,
He was a man born with thy face and throat,
    Lyric Apollo!
Long he lived nameless: how should spring take note
    Winter would follow?
Till lo, the little touch, and youth was gone!
    Cramped and diminished,
Moaned he, "New measures, other feet anon!
    My dance is finished?"
No, that's the world's way; (keep the mountain-side,
    Make for the city!)
He knew the signal, and stepped on with pride
    Over men's pity;
Left play for work, and grappled with the world
    Bent on escaping:
"What's in the scroll," quoth he, "thou keepest furled?
    Show me their shaping,

Theirs who most studied man, the bard and sage,—
    Give!"—So, he gowned him,
Straight got by heart that book to its last page:
    Learned, we found him.
Yea, but we found him bald too, eyes like lead,
    Accents uncertain:
"Time to taste life," another would have said,
    "Up with the curtain!"
This man said rather, "Actual life comes next?
    Patience a moment!
Grant I have mastered learning's crabbed text,
    Still there's the comment.
Let me know all! Prate not of most or least,
    Painful or easy!
Even to the crumbs I'd fain eat up the feast,
    Ay, nor feel queasy."
Oh, such a life as he resolved to live,
    When he had learned it,
When he had gathered all books had to give!
    Sooner, he spurned it.
Image the whole, then execute the parts—
    Fancy the fabric
Quite, ere you build, ere steel strike fire from quartz,
    Ere mortar dab brick!

(Here's the town-gate reached; there's the market-place
    Gaping before us.)
Yea, this in him was the peculiar grace
    (Hearten our chorus!)
That before living he'd learn how to live—
    No end to learning:
Earn the means first—God surely will contrive
    Use for our earning.
Others mistrust and say, "But time escapes!
    Live now or never!"
He said, "What's time? Leave Now for dogs and apes!
    Man has Forever."
Back to his book then: deeper drooped his head:
    Calculus[1] racked him:
Leaden before, his eyes grew dross of lead:

---

[1] Gallstones.

Tussis[2] attacked him.
"Now, master, take a little rest!"—not he!
    (Caution redoubled!
Step two abreast, the way winds narrowly!)
        Not a whit troubled,
Back to his studies, fresher than at first,
        Fierce as a dragon
He (soul-hydroptic with a sacred thirst)
        Sucked at the flagon.
Oh, if we draw a circle premature,
        Heedless of far gain,
Greedy for quick returns of profit, sure
        Bad is our bargain!
Was it not great? did not he throw on God
        (He loves the burthen)—
God's task to make the heavenly period
        Perfect the earthen?
Did not he magnify the mind, show clear
        Just what it all meant?
He would not discount life, as fools do here,
        Paid by instalment.
He ventured neck or nothing—heaven's success
        Found, or earth's failure:
"Wilt thou trust death or not?" He answered "Yes!
        Hence with life's pale lure!"
That low man seeks a little thing to do,
        Sees it and does it:
This high man, with a great thing to pursue,
        Dies ere he knows it.
That low man goes on adding one to one,
        His hundred's soon hit:
This high man, aiming at a million,
        Misses an unit.
That, has the world here—should he need the next,
        Let the world mind him!
This, throws himself on God, and unperplexed
        Seeking shall find him.
So, with the throttling hands of death at strife,
        Ground he at grammar;

_____
[2] Coughing.

Still, thro' the rattle, parts of speech were rife:
    While he could stammer
He settled *Hoti's* business—let it be!—
    Properly based *Oun*—
Gave us the doctrine of the enclitic *De*, [3]
    Dead from the waist down.
Well, here's the platform, here's the proper place:
    Hail to your purlieus,
All ye highfliers of the feathered race,
    Swallows and curlews!
Here's the top-peak; the multitude below
    Live, for they can, there:
This man decided not to Live but Know—
    Bury this man there?
Here—here's his place, where meteors shoot, clouds form,
    Lightnings are loosened,
Stars come and go! Let joy break with the storm,
    Peace let the dew send!
Lofty designs must close in like effects:
    Loftily lying,
Leave him—still loftier than. the world suspects,
    Living and dying.

Dîs Aliter Visum; or, Le Byron de Nos Jours [2]

I   Stop, let me have the truth of that!
      Is that all true? I say, the day
   Ten years ago when both of us
      Met on a morning, friends—as thus
   We meet this evening, friends or what?—

II   Did you—because I took your arm
      And sillily smiled, "A mass of brass

---

[1] *Hoti* and *oun* are Greek words meaning "what" and "well, then"; *de* is a suffix meaning "toward."

[2] "The gods thought otherwise; or, the Byron of our time."

That sea looks, blazing underneath!"
    While up the cliff-road edged with heath,
We took the turns nor came to harm—

III Did you consider "Now makes twice
    That I have seen her, walked and talked
With this poor pretty thoughtful thing,
    Whose worth I weigh: she tries to sing;
Draws, hopes in time the eye grows nice;

IV "Reads verse and thinks she understands;
    Loves all, at any rate, that's great,
Good, beautiful; but much as we
    Down at the bath-house love the sea,
Who breathe its salt and bruise its sands:

V "While . . . do but follow the fishing-gull
    That flaps and floats from wave to cave!
There's the sea-lover, fair my friend!
    What then? Be patient, mark and mend!
Had you the making of your skull?"

VI And did you, when we faced the church
    With spire and sad slate roof, aloof
From human fellowship so far,
    Where a few graveyard crosses are,
And garlands for the swallows' perch,—

VII Did you determine, as we stepped
    O'er the lone stone fence, "Let me get
Her for myself, and what's the earth
    With all its art, verse, music, worth—
Compared with love, found, gained, and kept?

VIII "Schumann's our music-maker now;
    Has his march-movement youth and mouth?
Ingres's the modern man that paints;
    Which will lean on me, of his saints?
Heine for songs; for kisses, how?"

IX   And did you, when we entered, reached
    The votive frigate, soft aloft
Riding on air this hundred years,
    Safe-smiling at old hopes and fears,—
Did you draw profit while she preached?

X   Resolving, "Fools we wise men grow:
    Yes, I could easily blurt out curt
Some question that might find reply
    As prompt in her stopped lips, dropped eye
And rush of red to cheek and brow:

XI   "Thus were a match made, sure and fast,
    'Mid the blue weed-flowers round the mound
Where, issuing, we shall stand and stay
    For one more look at baths and bay,
Sands, sea-gulls, and the old church last—

XII   "A match 'twixt me, bent, wigged and lamed,
    Famous, however, for verse and worse,
Sure of the Fortieth spare Arm-chair[1]
    When gout and glory seat me there,
So, one whose love-freaks pass unblamed,—

XIII   "And this young beauty, round and sound
    As a mountain-apple, youth and truth
With loves and doves, at all events
    With money in the Three per Cents;[2]
Whose choice of me would seem profound:—

XIV   "She might take me as I take her.
    Perfect the hour would pass, alas!
Climb high, love high, what matter? Still,
    Feet, feelings, must descend the hill:
An hour's perfection can't recur.

XV   "Then follows Paris and full time
    For both to reason: 'Thus with us,'
She'll sigh, 'Thus girls give body and soul

---

[1] Sure of election to the French Academy.
[2] Safe government bonds.

At first word, think they gain the goal,
When 't is the starting-place they climb!

XVI   " 'My friend makes verse and gets renown;
Have they all fifty years, his peers?
He knows the world, firm, quiet and gay;
Boys will become as much one day:
They're fools; he cheats, with beard less brown.

XVII   " 'For boys say, *Love me or I die!*
He did not say, *The truth is, youth
I want, who am old and know too much;
I'd catch youth: lend me sight and touch!
Drop heart's blood where life's wheels grate dry!*'

XVIII   "While I should make rejoinder"—(then
It was, no doubt, you ceased that least
Light pressure of my arm in yours)
I can conceive of cheaper cures
For a yawning-fit o'er books and men.

XIX   " 'What? All I am, was, and might be,
All, books taught, art brought, life's whole strife,
Painful results since precious, just
Were fitly exchanged, in wise disgust,
For two cheeks freshened by youth and sea?

XX   " 'All for a nosegay!—what came first;
With fields in flower, untried each side;
I rally, need my books and men,
And find a nosegay:' drop it, then,
No match yet made for best or worst!"

XXI   That ended me. You judged the porch
We left by, Norman; took our look
At sea and sky; wondered so few
Find out the place for air and view;
Remarked the sun began to scorch;

XXII   Descended, soon regained the baths,
And then, good-bye! Years ten since then:
Ten years! We meet: you tell me, now,

By a window-seat for that cliff-brow,
On carpet-stripes for those sand-paths.

XXIII   Now I may speak: you fool, for all
              Your lore! WHO made things plain in vain?
          What was the sea for? What, the gray
              Sad church, that solitary day,
          Crosses and graves and swallows' call?

XXIV   Was there naught better than to enjoy?
              No feat which, done, would make time break
          And let us pent-up creatures through
              Into eternity, our due?
          No forcing earth teach heaven's employ?

XXV   No wise beginning, here and now,
              What cannot grow complete (earth's feat)
          And heaven must finish, there and then?
              No tasting earth's true food for men,
          Its sweet in sad, its sad in sweet?

XXVI   No grasping at love, gaining a share
              O' the sole spark from God's life at strife
          With death, so, sure of range above
              The limits here? For us and love,
          Failure; but, when God fails, despair.

XXVII This you call wisdom? Thus you add
              Good unto good again, in vain?
          You loved, with body worn and weak;
              I loved, with faculties to seek:
          Were both loves worthless since ill-clad?

XXVIII Let the mere star-fish in his vault
              Crawl in a wash of weed, indeed,
          Rose-jacynth to the finger-tips:
              He, whole in body and soul, outstrips
          Man, found with either in default.

xxix But what's whole, can increase no more,
          Is dwarfed and dies, since here's its sphere.
      The devil laughed at you in his sleeve!
          You knew not? That I well believe;
      Or you had saved two souls: nay, four.

xxx   For Stephanie sprained last night her wrist,
          Ankle or something. "Pooh," cry you?
      At any rate she danced, all say,
          Vilely; her vogue has had its day.
      Here comes my husband from his whist.

Caliban upon Setebos; or, Natural Theology in the Island[1]

"Thou thoughtest that I was altogether such a one as thyself."

['Will sprawl, now that the heat of day is best,
Flat on his belly in the pit's much mire,
With elbows wide, fists clenched to prop his chin,
And, while he kicks both feet in the cool slush,
And feels about his spine small eft-things course,
Run in and out each arm, and make him laugh:
And while above his head a pompion-plant,[2]
Coating the cave-top as a brow its eye,
Creeps down to touch and tickle hair and beard,
And now a flower drops with a bee inside,
And now a fruit to snap at, catch and crunch,—
He looks out o'er yon sea which sunbeams cross
And recross till they weave a spider-web,
(Meshes of fire, some great fish breaks at times)
And talks to his own self, howe'er he please,
Touching that other, whom his dam called God.
Because to talk about Him, vexes—ha,

---

[1] Caliban is the primitive man-beast in Shakespeare's *The Tempest*; his mother, the witch Sycorax, worshiped the god Setebos.
[2] Pumpkin.

Could He but know! and time to vex is now,
When talk is safer than in winter-time.
Moreover Prosper and Miranda[1] sleep
In confidence he drudges at their task,
And it is good to cheat the pair, and gibe,
Letting the rank tongue blossom into speech.]

   Setebos, Setebos, and Setebos!
'Thinketh, He dwelleth i' the cold o' the moon.

'Thinketh He made it, with the sun to match,
But not the stars; the stars came otherwise;
Only made clouds, winds, meteors, such as that:
Also this isle, what lives and grows thereon,
And snaky sea which rounds and ends the same.

'Thinketh, it came of being ill at ease:
He hated that He can not change His cold,
Nor cure its ache. 'Hath spied an icy fish
That longed to 'scape the rock-stream where she lived,
And thaw herself within the lukewarm brine
O' the lazy sea her stream thrusts far amid,
A crystal spike 'twixt two warm walls of wave;
Only, she ever sickened, found repulse
At the other kind of water, not her life,
(Green-dense and dim-delicious, bred o' the sun)
Flounced back from bliss she was not born to breathe,
And in her old bounds buried her despair,
Hating and loving warmth alike: so He.

'Thinketh, He made thereat the sun, this isle,
Trees and the fowls here, beast and creeping thing.
Yon otter, sleek-wet, black, lithe as a leech;
Yon auk, one fire-eye in a ball of foam,
That floats and feeds; a certain badger brown,
He hath watched hunt with that slant white-wedge eye
By moonlight; and the pie with the long tongue
That pricks deep into oakwarts for a worm,
And says a plain word when she finds her prize,
But will not eat the ants; the ants themselves
That build a wall of seeds and settled stalks

---

[1] Characters in *The Tempest*.

About their hole—He made all these and more,
Made all we see, and us, in spite: how else?
He could not, Himself, make a second self
To be His mate: as well have made Himself:
He would not make what He mislikes or slights,
An eyesore to Him, or not worth His pains;
But did, in envy, listlessness or sport,
Make what Himself would fain, in a manner, be—
Weaker in most points, stronger in a few,
Worthy, and yet mere playthings all the while,
Things He admires and mocks too,—that is it!
Because, so brave, so better tho' they be,
It nothing skills if He begin to plague.
Look now, I melt a gourd-fruit into mash,
Add honeycomb and pods, I have perceived,
Which bite like finches when they bill and kiss,—
Then, when froth rises bladdery, drink up all,
Quick, quick, till maggots scamper thro' my brain;
Last, throw me on my back i' the seeded thyme,
And wanton, wishing I were born a bird.
Put case, unable to be what I wish,
I yet could make a live bird out of clay:
Would not I take clay, pinch my Caliban
Able to fly?—for, there, see, he hath wings,
And great comb like the hoopoe's to admire,
And there, a sting to do his foes offence,
There, and I will that he begin to live,
Fly to yon rock-top, nip me off the horns
Of grigs[1] high up that make the merry din,
Saucy thro' their veined wings, and mind me not.
In which feat, if his leg snapped, brittle clay,
And he lay stupid-like,—why, I should laugh;
And if he, spying me, should fall to weep,
Beseech me to be good, repair his wrong,
Bid his poor leg smart less or grow again,—
Well, as the chance were, this might take or else
Not take my fancy: I might hear his cry,
And give the mankin three sound legs for one,
Or pluck the other off, leave him like an egg,

---

[1] Crickets.

And lessoned he was mine and merely clay.
Were this no pleasure, lying in the thyme,
Drinking the mash, with brain become alive,
Making and marring clay at will? So He.

'Thinketh, such shows nor right nor wrong in Him
Nor kind, nor cruel: He is strong and Lord.
'Am strong myself compared to yonder crabs
That march now from the mountain to the sea;
'Let twenty pass, and stone the twenty-first,
Loving not, hating not, just choosing so.
'Say, the first straggler that boasts purple spots
Shall join the file, one pincer twisted off;
'Say, this bruised fellow shall receive a worm,
And two worms he whose nippers end in red:
As it likes me each time, I do: so He.

Well then, 'supposeth He is good i' the main,
Placable if His mind and ways were guessed,
But rougher than His handiwork, be sure!
Oh, He hath made things worthier than Himself,
And envieth that, so helped, such things do more
Than He who made them! What consoles but this?
That they, unless thro' Him, do naught at all,
And must submit: what other use in things?
'Hath cut a pipe of pithless elder-joint
That, blown through, gives exact the scream o' the jay
When from her wing you twitch the feathers blue:
Sound this, and little birds that hate the jay
Flock within stone's throw, glad their foe is hurt:
Put case such pipe could prattle and boast forsooth
"I catch the birds, I am the crafty thing,
I make the cry my maker can not make
With his great round mouth; he must blow thro' mine!"
Would not I smash it with my foot? So He.

    But wherefore rough, why cold and ill at ease?
Aha, that is a question! Ask, for that,
What knows,—the something over Setebos
That made Him, or He, may be, found and fought,
Worsted, drove off and did to nothing, perchance.
There may be something quiet o'er His head,

Out of His reach, that feels nor joy nor grief,
Since both derive from weakness in some way.
I joy because the quails come; would not joy
Could I bring quails here when I have a mind:
This Quiet, all it hath a mind to, doth.
'Esteemeth stars the outposts of its couch,
But never spends much thought nor care that way.
It may look up, work up,—the worse for those
It works on! 'Careth but for Setebos
The many-handed as a cuttle-fish,
Who, making Himself feared thro' what He does,
Looks up, first, and perceives he can not soar
To what is quiet and hath happy life;
Next looks down here, and out of very spite
Makes this a bauble-world to ape yon real,
These good things to match those as hips do grapes.
'T is solace making baubles, ay, and sport.
Himself peeped late, eyed Prosper at his books
Careless and lofty, lord now of the isle:
Vexed, 'stitched a book of broad leaves, arrow-shaped,
Wrote thereon, he knows what, prodigious words;
Has peeled a wand and called it by a name;
Weareth at whiles for an enchanter's robe
The eyed skin of a supple oncelot;[1]
And hath an ounce sleeker than youngling mole,
A four-legged serpent he makes cower and couch,
Now snarl, now hold its breath and mind his eye,
And saith she is Miranda and my wife:
'Keeps for his Ariel[2] a tall pouch-bill crane
He bids go wade for fish and straight disgorge;
Also a sea-beast, lumpish, which he snared,
Blinded the eyes of, and brought somewhat tame,
And split its toe-webs, and now pens the drudge
In a hole o' the rock, and calls him Caliban;
A bitter heart that bides its time and bites.
'Plays thus at being Prosper in a way,
Taketh his mirth with make-believes: so He.

---

[1] Ocelot.
[2] The spirit who is commanded by Prospero in *The Tempest*.

His dam held that the Quiet made all things
Which Setebos vexed only: 'holds not so.
Who made them weak, meant weakness He might vex.
Had He meant other, while His hand was in,
Why not make horny eyes no thorn could prick,
Or plate my scalp with bone against the snow,
Or overscale my flesh 'neath joint and joint,
Like an orc's[1] armour? Ay,—so spoil His sport!
He is the One now: only He doth all.

'Saith, He may like, perchance, what profits Him.
Ay, himself loves what does him good; but why?
'Gets good no otherwise. This blinded beast
Loves whoso places flesh-meat on his nose,
But, had he eyes, would want no help, but hate
Or love, just as it liked him: He hath eyes.
Also it pleaseth Setebos to work,
Use all His hands, and exercise much craft,
By no means for the love of what is worked.
'Tasteth, himself, no finer good i' the world
When all goes right, in this safe summer-time,
And he wants little, hungers, aches not much,
Than trying what to do with wit and strength.
'Falls to make something: 'piled yon pile of turfs,
And squared and stuck there squares of soft white chalk,
And, with a fish-tooth, scratched a moon on each,
And set up endwise certain spikes of tree,
And crowned the whole with a sloth's skull a-top,
Found dead i' the woods, too hard for one to kill.
No use at all i' the work, for work's sole sake;
'Shall some day knock it down again: so He.

'Saith He is terrible: watch His feats in proof!
One hurricane will spoil six good months' hope.
He hath a spite against me, that I know.
Just as He favours Prosper, who knows why?
So it is, all the same, as well I find.
'Wove wattles half the winter, fenced them firm
With stone and stake to stop she-tortoises
Crawling to lay their eggs here: well, one wave,
Feeling the foot of Him upon its neck,

---

[1] Sea monster's.

Gaped as a snake does, lolled out its large tongue,
And licked the whole labour flat: so much for spite!
'Saw a ball flame down late (yonder it lies)
Where, half an hour before, I slept i' the shade:
Often they scatter sparkles: there is force!
'Dug up a newt He may have envied once
And turned to stone, shut up inside a stone.
Please Him and hinder this?—What Prosper does?
Aha, if he would tell me how. Not He!
There is the sport: discover how or die!
All need not die, for of the things o' the isle
Some flee afar, some dive, some run up trees;
Those at His mercy,—why, they please Him most
When . . . when . . . well, never try the same way twice!
Repeat what act has pleased, He may grow wroth.
You must not know His ways, and play Him off,
Sure of the issue. 'Doth the like himself:
'Spareth a squirrel that it nothing fears
But steals the nut from underneath my thumb,
And when I threat, bites stoutly in defence:
'Spareth an urchin[1] that contrariwise,
Curls up into a ball, pretending death
For fright at my approach: the two ways please.
But what would move my choler more than this,
That either creature counted on its life
To-morrow, next day and all days to come,
Saying forsooth in the inmost of its heart,
"Because he did so yesterday with me,
And otherwise with such another brute,
So must he do henceforth and always." Ay?
'Would teach the reasoning couple what "must" means!
'Doth as he likes, or wherefore Lord? So He.

'Conceiveth all things will continue thus,
And we shall have to live in fear of Him
So long as He lives, keeps His strength: no change,
If He have done His best, make no new world
To please Him more, so leave off watching this,—
If He surprise not even the Quiet's self
Some strange day,—or, suppose, grow into it

---

[1] Hedgehog.

As grubs grow butterflies: else, here are we,
And there is He, and nowhere help at all.

'Believeth with the life the pain shall stop.
His dam held different, that after death
He both plagued enemies and feasted friends:
Idly! He doth His worst in this our life,
Giving just respite lest we die thro' pain,
Saving last pain for worst,—with which, an end.
Meanwhile, the best way to escape His ire
Is, not to seem too happy. 'Sees, himself,
Yonder two flies, with purple films and pink,
Bask on the pompion-bell above: kills both.
'Sees two black painful beetles roll their ball
On head and tail as if to save their lives:
'Moves them the stick away they strive to clear.

Even so, 'would have Him misconceive, suppose
This Caliban strives hard and ails no less,
And always, above all else, envies Him;
Wherefore he mainly dances on dark nights,
Moans in the sun, gets under holes to laugh,
And never speaks his mind save housed as now:
Outside, 'groans, curses. If He caught me here,
O'erheard this speech, and asked "What chucklest at?"
'Would, to appease Him, cut a finger off,
Or of my three kid yearlings burn the best,
Or let the toothsome apples rot on tree,
Or push my tame beast for the orc to taste:
While myself lit a fire, and made a song
And sung it, *"What I hate, be consecrate*
To celebrate Thee and Thy state, no mate
For Thee; what see for envy in poor me?"
Hoping the while, since evils sometimes mend,
Warts rub away and sores are cured with slime,
That some strange day, will either the Quiet catch
And conquer Setebos, or likelier He
Decrepit may doze, doze, as good as die.

[What, what? A curtain o'er the world at once!
Crickets stop hissing; not a bird—or, yes,
There scuds His raven that hath told Him all!

It was fool's play, this prattling! Ha! The wind
Shoulders the pillared dust, death's house o' the move,
And fast invading fires begin! White blaze—
A tree's head snaps—and there, there, there, there, there,
His thunder follows! Fool to give at Him!
Lo! 'Lieth flat and loveth Setebos!
'Maketh his teeth meet thro' his upper lip,
Will let those quails fly, will not eat this month
One little mess of whelks, so he may 'scape!]

Confessions

I   What is he buzzing in my ears?
        "Now that I come to die,
    Do I view the world as a vale of tears?"
        Ah, reverend sir, not I!

II   What I viewed there once, what I view again
        Where the physic bottles stand
    On the table's edge,—is a suburb lane,
        With a wall to my bedside hand.

III   That lane sloped, much as the bottles do,
        From a house you could descry
    O'er the garden-wall: is the curtain blue
        Or green to a healthy eye?

IV   To mine, it serves for the old June weather
        Blue above lane and wall;
    And that farthest bottle labeled "Ether"
        Is the house o'er-topping all.

V   At a terrace, somewhere near the stopper,
        There watched for me, one June,
    A girl: I know, sir, it's improper,
        My poor mind's out of tune.

VI   Only, there was a way . . . you crept
      Close by the side, to dodge
    Eyes in the house, two eyes except:
      They styled their house "The Lodge."

VII   What right had a lounger up their lane?
      But, by creeping very close,
    With the good wall's help,—their eyes might strain
      And stretch themselves to Oes,

VIII   Yet never catch her and me together,
      As she left the attic, there,
    By the rim of the bottle labeled "Ether,"
      And stole from stair to stair,

IX   And stood by the rose-wreathed gate. Alas,
      We loved, sir—used to meet:
    How sad and bad and mad it was—
      But then, how it was sweet!

Youth and Art

I   It once might have been, once only:
      We lodged in a street together,
    You, a sparrow on the housetop lonely,
      I, a lone she-bird of his feather.

II   Your trade was with sticks and clay,
      You thumbed, thrust, patted and polished,
    Then laughed "They will see, some day,
      Smith made, and Gibson[1] demolished."

III   My business was song, song, song;
      I chirped, cheeped, trilled and twittered,
    "Kate Brown's on the boards ere long,
      And Grisi's[2] existence embittered!"

---

[1] John Gibson, nineteenth-century English sculptor.
[2] Giulia Grisi, Italian opera singer.

IV I earned no more by a warble
        Than you by a sketch in plaster;
    You wanted a piece of marble,
        I needed a music-master.

V   We studied hard in our styles,
        Chipped each at a crust like Hindoos,
    For air, looked out on the tiles,
        For fun, watched each other's windows.

VI You lounged, like a boy of the South,
        Cap and blouse—nay, a bit of beard too;
    Or you got it, rubbing your mouth
        With fingers the clay adhered to.

VII And I—soon managed to find
        Weak points in the flower-fence facing,
    Was forced to put up a blind
        And be safe in my corset-lacing.

VIII No harm! It was not my fault
        If you never turned your eye's tail up
    As I shook upon E *in alt*,[1]
        Or ran the chromatic scale up:

IX For spring bade the sparrows pair,
        And the boys and girls gave guesses,
    And stalls in our street looked rare
        With bulrush and watercresses.

X   Why did not you pinch a flower
        In a pellet of clay and fling it?
    Why did not I put a power
        Of thanks in a look, or sing it?

XI I did look, sharp as a lynx,
        (And yet the memory rankles)
    When models arrived, some minx
        Tripped up stairs, she and her ankles.

[1] Trilled a high E.

XII   But I think I gave you as good!
     "That foreign fellow,—who can know
   How she pays, in a playful mood,
     For his tuning her that piano?"

XIII   Could you say so, and never say
     "Suppose we join hands and fortunes,
   And I fetch her from over the way,
     Her, piano, and long tunes and short tunes?"

XIV   No, no: you would not be rash,
     Nor I rasher and something over;
   You've to settle yet Gibson's hash,
     And Grisi yet lives in clover.

XV   But you meet the Prince at the Board,
     I'm queen myself at *bals-parés*, [1]
   I've married a rich old lord,
     And you're dubbed knight and an R.A. [2]

XVI   Each life unfulfilled, you see;
     It hangs still, patchy and scrappy:
   We have not sighed deep, laughed free,
     Starved, feasted, despaired,—been happy.

XVII   And nobody calls you a dunce,
     And people suppose me clever;
   This could but have happened once,
     And we missed it, lost it for ever.

Apparent Failure

"We shall soon lose a celebrated building."
PARIS NEWSPAPER

I   No, for I'll save it! Seven years since,
     I passed thro' Paris, stopped a day

---

[1] Full-dress balls.
[2] Member of the Royal Academy.

To see the baptism of your Prince;
    Saw, made my bow, and went my way:
Walking the heat and headache off,
    I took the Seine-side, you surmise,
Thought of the Congress, Gortschakoff,
    Cavour's appeal and Buol's replies,[1]
So sauntered till—what met my eyes?

II   Only the Doric little Morgue!
    The dead-house where you show your drowned:
Petrarch's Vaucluse makes proud the Sorgue,[2]
    Your Morgue has made the Seine renowned.
One pays one's debt in such a case;
    I plucked up heart and entered,—stalked,
Keeping a tolerable face
    Compared with some whose cheeks were chalked:
Let them! No Briton's to be balked!

III   First came the silent gazers; next,
    A screen of glass, we're thankful for;
Last, the sight's self, the sermon's text,
    The three men who did most abhor
Their life in Paris yesterday,
    So killed themselves: and now, enthroned
Each on his copper couch, they lay
    Fronting me, waiting to be owned.
I thought, and think, their sin's atoned.

IV   Poor men, God made, and all for that!
    The reverence struck me; o'er each head
Religiously was hung its hat,
    Each coat dripped by the owner's bed,
Sacred from touch: each had his berth,
    His bounds, his proper place of rest,
Who last night tenanted on earth
    Some arch, where twelve such slept abreast,—
Unless the plain asphalt seemed best.

---

[1] Gortschakoff was the Russian representative at the Paris congress negotiating the end of the Crimean War. Count Cavour, Prime Minister of Austria, and Count Buol-Schauenstein, the Austrian representative, were other important figures at the congress.
[2] Petrarch lived at Fontaine-de-Vaucluse, in Provence, at the source of the Sorgue river.

v   How did it happen, my poor boy?
        You wanted to be Buonaparte
    And have the Tuileries for toy,
        And could not, so it broke your heart?
    You, old one by his side, I judge,
        Were, red as blood, a socialist,
    A leveller! Does the Empire grudge
        You've gained what no Republic missed?
    Be quiet, and unclench your fist!

vi And this—why, he was red in vain,
        Or black,—poor fellow that is blue!
    What fancy was it, turned your brain?
        Oh, women were the prize for you!
    Money gets women, cards and dice
        Get money, and ill-luck gets just
    The copper couch and one clear nice
        Cool squirt of water o'er your bust,
    The right thing to extinguish lust!

vii It's wiser being good than bad;
        It's safer being meek than fierce:
    It's fitter being sane than mad.
        My own hope is, a sun will pierce
    The thickest cloud earth ever stretched;
        That, after Last, returns the First,
    Tho' a wide compass round be fetched;
        That what began best, can't end worst,
    Nor what God blessed once, prove accurst.

House

i   Shall I sonnet-sing you about myself?
        Do I live in a house you would like to see?
    Is it scant of gear, has it store of pelf?
        "Unlock my heart with a sonnet-key?"

ii Invite the world, as my betters have done?
        "Take notice: this building remains on view,

Its suites of reception every one,
    Its private apartment and bedroom too;

III   "For a ticket, apply to the Publisher."
    No: thanking the public, I must decline.
A peep thro' my window, if folk prefer;
    But, please you, no foot over threshold of mine!

IV   I have mixed with a crowd and heard free talk
    In a foreign land where an earthquake chanced,
And a house stood gaping, naught to balk
    Man's eye wherever he gazed or glanced.

V   The whole of the frontage shaven sheer,
    The inside gaped: exposed to day,
Right and wrong and common and queer,
    Bare, as the palm of your hand, it lay.

VI   The owner? Oh, he had been crushed, no doubt!
    "Odd tables and chairs for a man of wealth!
What a parcel of musty old books about!
    He smoked,—no wonder he lost his health!

VII   "I doubt if he bathed before he dressed.
    A brasier?—the pagan, he burned perfumes!
You see it is proved, what the neighbours guessed:
    His wife and himself had separate rooms."

VIII   Friends, the goodman of the house at least
    Kept house to himself till an earthquake came:
'T is the fall of its frontage permits you feast
    On the inside arrangement you praise or blame.

IX   Outside should suffice for evidence:
    And whoso desires to penetrate
Deeper, must dive by the spirit-sense—
    No optics like yours, at any rate!

X   "Hoity toity! A street to explore,
    Your house the exception! 'With this same key
Shakespeare unlocked his heart,' once more!"
    Did Shakespeare? If so, the less Shakespeare he!

Wanting Is—What?

Wanting is—what?
Summer redundant,
Blueness abundant,
—Where is the blot?
Beamy the world, yet a blank all the same,
—Framework which waits for a picture to frame:
What of the leafage, what of the flower?
Roses embowering with naught they embower!
Come then, complete incompletion, O comer,
Pant thro' the blueness, perfect the summer!
Breathe but one breath
Rose-beauty above,
And all that was death
Grows life, grows love,
Grows love!

Never the Time and the Place

Never the time and the place
And the loved one all together!
This path—how soft to pace!
This May—what magic weather!
Where is the loved one's face?
In a dream that loved one's face meets mine,
But the house is narrow, the place is bleak
Where, outside, rain and wind combine
With a furtive ear, if I strive to speak,
With a hostile eye at my flushing cheek,
With a malice that marks each word, each sign!
O enemy sly and serpentine,
Uncoil thee from the waking man!
Do I hold the Past
Thus firm and fast
Yet doubt if the Future hold I can?

This path so soft to pace shall lead
Thro' the magic of May to herself indeed!
Or narrow if needs the house must be,
Outside are the storms and strangers: we—
Oh, close, safe, warm sleep I and she,
—I and she!

The Names

Shakespeare!—to such name's sounding, what succeeds
    Fitly as silence? Falter forth the spell,—
    Act follows word, the speaker knows full well,
Nor tampers with its magic more than needs.
Two names there are: That which the Hebrew reads
    With his soul only: if from lips it fell,
    Echo, back thundered by earth, heaven, and hell,
Would own "Thou didst create us!" Naught impedes
We voice the other name, man's most of might,
    Awesomely, lovingly: let awe and love
Mutely await their working, leave to sight
    All of the issue as—below—above—
Shakespeare's creation rises: one remove,
Tho' dread—this finite from that infinite.

Why I Am a Liberal

"Why?" Because all I haply can and do,
    All that I am now, all I hope to be,—
    Whence comes it save from fortune setting free
Body and soul the purpose to pursue,
God traced for both? If fetters, not a few,
    Of prejudice, convention, fall from me,
    These shall I bid men—each in his degree
Also God-guided—bear, and gayly too?

But little do or can the best of us:
That little is achieved thro' Liberty.
    Who then dares hold, emancipated thus,
His fellow shall continue bound? not I,
    Who live, love, labour freely, nor discuss
A brother's right to freedom. That is "Why."

Alphabetical List of Titles

Alphabetical List of First Lines

DOVER · THRIFT · EDITIONS

All books complete and unabridged. All 5³⁄₁₆″ × 8¹⁄₄″, paperbound.
Just $1.00–$2.00 in U.S.A.

POETRY

DOVER BEACH AND OTHER POEMS, Matthew Arnold. 112pp. 28037-3 $1.00

BHAGAVADGITA, Bhagavadgita. 112pp. 27782-8 $1.00

SONGS OF INNOCENCE AND SONGS OF EXPERIENCE, William Blake. 64pp. 27051-3 $1.00

SONNETS FROM THE PORTUGUESE AND OTHER POEMS, Elizabeth Barrett Browning. 64pp. 27052-1 $1.00

MY LAST DUCHESS AND OTHER POEMS, Robert Browning. 128pp. 27783-6 $1.00

POEMS AND SONGS, Robert Burns. 96pp. 26863-2 $1.00

SELECTED POEMS, George Gordon, Lord Byron. 112pp. 27784-4 $1.00

THE RIME OF THE ANCIENT MARINER AND OTHER POEMS, Samuel Taylor Coleridge. 80pp. 27266-4 $1.00

SELECTED POEMS, Emily Dickinson. 64pp. 26466-1 $1.00

SELECTED POEMS, John Donne. 96pp. 27788-7 $1.00

THE RUBÁIYÁT OF OMAR KHAYYÁM: FIRST AND FIFTH EDITIONS, Edward FitzGerald. 64pp. 26467-X $1.00

A BOY'S WILL AND NORTH OF BOSTON, Robert Frost. 112pp. (Available in U.S. only.) 26866-7 $1.00

THE ROAD NOT TAKEN AND OTHER POEMS, Robert Frost. 64pp. (Available in U.S. only) 27550-7 $1.00

A SHROPSHIRE LAD, A. E. Housman. 64pp. 26468-8 $1.00

LYRIC POEMS, John Keats. 80pp. 26871-3 $1.00

THE BOOK OF PSALMS, King James Bible. 128pp. 27541-8 $1.00

GUNGA DIN AND OTHER FAVORITE POEMS, Rudyard Kipling. 80pp. 26471-8 $1.00

THE CONGO AND OTHER POEMS, Vachel Lindsay. 96pp. 27272-9 $1.00

FAVORITE POEMS, Henry Wadsworth Longfellow. 96pp. 27273-7 $1.00

SPOON RIVER ANTHOLOGY, Edgar Lee Masters. 144pp. 27275-3 $1.00

RENASCENCE AND OTHER POEMS, Edna St. Vincent Millay. 64pp. (Available in U.S. only.) 26873-X $1.00

SELECTED POEMS, John Milton. 128pp. 27554-X $1.00

GREAT SONNETS, Paul Negri (ed.). 96pp. 28052-7 $1.00

THE RAVEN AND OTHER FAVORITE POEMS, Edgar Allan Poe. 64pp. 26685-0 $1.00

ESSAY ON MAN AND OTHER POEMS, Alexander Pope. 128pp. 28053-5 $1.00

GOBLIN MARKET AND OTHER POEMS, Christina Rossetti. 64pp. 28055-1 $1.00

CHICAGO POEMS, Carl Sandburg. 80pp. 28057-8 $1.00

THE SHOOTING OF DAN MCGREW AND OTHER POEMS, Robert Service. 96pp. 27556-6 $1.00

COMPLETE SONGS FROM THE PLAYS, William Shakespeare. 80pp. 27801-8 $1.00

COMPLETE SONNETS, William Shakespeare. 80pp. 26686-9 $1.00

SELECTED POEMS, Percy Bysshe Shelley. 128pp. 27558-2 $1.00

SELECTED POEMS, Alfred Lord Tennyson. 112pp. 27282-6 $1.00

CHRISTMAS CAROLS: COMPLETE VERSES, Shane Weller (ed.). 64pp. 27397-0 $1.00

DOVER · THRIFT · EDITIONS

All books complete and unabridged. All 5³⁄₁₆″ × 8¼″, paperbound.
Just $1.00–$2.00 in U.S.A.

POETRY

GREAT LOVE POEMS, Shane Weller (ed.). 128pp. 27284-2 $1.00

SELECTED POEMS, Walt Whitman. 128pp. 26878-0 $1.00

THE BALLAD OF READING GAOL AND OTHER POEMS, Oscar Wilde. 64pp. 27072-6 $1.00

FAVORITE POEMS, William Wordsworth. 80pp. 27073-4 $1.00

EARLY POEMS, William Butler Yeats. 128pp. 27808-5 $1.00

FICTION

FLATLAND: A ROMANCE OF MANY DIMENSIONS, Edwin A. Abbott. 96pp. 27263-X $1.00

BEOWULF, Beowulf (trans. by R. K. Gordon). 64pp. 27264-8 $1.00

CIVIL WAR STORIES, Ambrose Bierce. 128pp. 28038-1 $1.00

ALICE'S ADVENTURES IN WONDERLAND, Lewis Carroll. 96pp. 27543-4 $1.00

O PIONEERS!, Willa Cather. 128pp. 27785-2 $1.00

FIVE GREAT SHORT STORIES, Anton Chekhov. 96pp. 26463-7 $1.00

FAVORITE FATHER BROWN STORIES, G. K. Chesterton. 96pp. 27545-0 $1.00

THE AWAKENING, Kate Chopin. 128pp. 27786-0 $1.00

HEART OF DARKNESS, Joseph Conrad. 80pp. 26464-5 $1.00

THE SECRET SHARER AND OTHER STORIES, Joseph Conrad. 128pp. 27546-9 $1.00

THE OPEN BOAT AND OTHER STORIES, Stephen Crane. 128pp. 27547-7 $1.00

THE RED BADGE OF COURAGE, Stephen Crane. 112pp. 26465-3 $1.00

A CHRISTMAS CAROL, Charles Dickens. 80pp. 26865-9 $1.00

THE CRICKET ON THE HEARTH AND OTHER CHRISTMAS STORIES, Charles Dickens. 128pp. 28039-X $1.00

NOTES FROM THE UNDERGROUND, Fyodor Dostoyevsky. 96pp. 27053-X $1.00

SIX GREAT SHERLOCK HOLMES STORIES, Sir Arthur Conan Doyle. 112pp. 27055-6 $1.00

WHERE ANGELS FEAR TO TREAD, E. M. Forster. 128pp. (Available in U.S. only) 27791-7 $1.00

THE OVERCOAT AND OTHER SHORT STORIES, Nikolai Gogol. 112pp. 27057-2 $1.00

GREAT GHOST STORIES, John Grafton (ed.). 112pp. 27270-2 $1.00

THE LUCK OF ROARING CAMP AND OTHER SHORT STORIES, Bret Harte. 96pp. 27271-0 $1.00

THE SCARLET LETTER, Nathaniel Hawthorne. 192pp. 28048-9 $2.00

YOUNG GOODMAN BROWN AND OTHER SHORT STORIES, Nathaniel Hawthorne. 128pp. 27060-2 $1.00

THE GIFT OF THE MAGI AND OTHER SHORT STORIES, O. Henry. 96pp. 27061-0 $1.00

THE NUTCRACKER AND THE GOLDEN POT, E. T. A. Hoffmann. 128pp. 27806-9 $1.00

THE BEAST IN THE JUNGLE AND OTHER STORIES, Henry James. 128pp. 27552-3 $1.00

THE TURN OF THE SCREW, Henry James. 96pp. 26684-2 $1.00

DUBLINERS, James Joyce. 160pp. 26870-5 $1.00

A PORTRAIT OF THE ARTIST AS A YOUNG MAN, James Joyce. 192pp. 28050-0 $2.00

DOVER · THRIFT · EDITIONS

All books complete and unabridged. All 5³/₁₆″ × 8¼″, paperbound.
Just $1.00–$2.00 in U.S.A.

FICTION

THE MAN WHO WOULD BE KING AND OTHER STORIES, Rudyard Kipling. 128pp. 28051-9
$1.00

SELECTED SHORT STORIES, D. H. Lawrence. 128pp. 27794-1 $1.00

GREEN TEA AND OTHER GHOST STORIES, J. Sheridan LeFanu. 96pp. 27795-X $1.00

THE CALL OF THE WILD, Jack London. 64pp. 26472-6 $1.00

FIVE GREAT SHORT STORIES, Jack London. 96pp. 27063-7 $1.00

WHITE FANG, Jack London. 160pp. 26968-X $1.00

THE NECKLACE AND OTHER SHORT STORIES, Guy de Maupassant. 128pp. 27064-5 $1.00

BARTLEBY AND BENITO CERENO, Herman Melville. 112pp. 26473-4 $1.00

THE GOLD-BUG AND OTHER TALES, Edgar Allan Poe. 128pp. 26875-6 $1.00

THE QUEEN OF SPADES AND OTHER STORIES, Alexander Pushkin. 128pp. 28054-3 $1.00

THREE LIVES, Gertrude Stein. 176pp. 28059-4 $2.00

THE STRANGE CASE OF DR. JEKYLL AND MR. HYDE, Robert Louis Stevenson. 64pp.
26688-5 $1.00

TREASURE ISLAND, Robert Louis Stevenson. 160pp. 27559-0 $1.00

THE KREUTZER SONATA AND OTHER SHORT STORIES, Leo Tolstoy. 144pp. 27805-0 $1.00

ADVENTURES OF HUCKLEBERRY FINN, Mark Twain. 224pp. 28061-6 $2.00

THE MYSTERIOUS STRANGER AND OTHER STORIES, Mark Twain. 128pp. 27069-6 $1.00

CANDIDE, Voltaire (François-Marie Arouet). 112pp. 26689-3 $1.00

THE INVISIBLE MAN, H. G. Wells. 112pp. (Available in U.S. only.) 27071-8 $1.00

ETHAN FROME, Edith Wharton. 96pp. 26690-7 $1.00

THE PICTURE OF DORIAN GRAY, Oscar Wilde. 192pp. 27807-7 $1.00

NONFICTION

THE DEVIL'S DICTIONARY, Ambrose Bierce. 144pp. 27542-6 $1.00

THE SOULS OF BLACK FOLK, W. E. B. Du Bois. 176pp. 28041-1 $2.00

SELF-RELIANCE AND OTHER ESSAYS, Ralph Waldo Emerson. 128pp. 27790-9 $1.00

GREAT SPEECHES, Abraham Lincoln. 112pp. 26872-1 $1.00

THE PRINCE, Niccolò Machiavelli. 80pp. 27274-5 $1.00

SYMPOSIUM AND PHAEDRUS, Plato. 96pp. 27798-4 $1.00

THE TRIAL AND DEATH OF SOCRATES: FOUR DIALOGUES, Plato. 128pp. 27066-1 $1.00

CIVIL DISOBEDIENCE AND OTHER ESSAYS, Henry David Thoreau. 96pp. 27563-9 $1.00

THE THEORY OF THE LEISURE CLASS, Thorstein Veblen. 256pp. 28062-4 $2.00

PLAYS

THE CHERRY ORCHARD, Anton Chekhov. 64pp. 26682-6 $1.00

THE THREE SISTERS, Anton Chekhov. 64pp. 27544-2 $1.00

THE WAY OF THE WORLD, William Congreve. 80pp. 27787-9 $1.00

MEDEA, Euripides. 64pp. 27548-5 $1.00

THE MIKADO, William Schwenck Gilbert. 64pp. 27268-0 $1.00